Catholics and Birth Control

Contemporary Views on Doctrine

BY DOROTHY DUNBAR BROMLEY

Foreword by Richard Cardinal Cushing
Preface by John L. Thomas, S.J.

THE DEVIN-ADAIR COMPANY
New York

Canadian Agents: Abelard-Schuman, Canada, Ltd., Toronto
Library of Congress Catalog Card Number: 64-23750

Manufactured in the United States of America
by H. Wolff, New York

Acknowledgments

1298628

Courteous permission was granted the author to quote, in some cases extensively, from:

"The Catholic Church and Birth Control," by Joseph S. Duhamel, S.J., one of a collection of essays entitled *In the Eyes of Others,* edited by Robert W. Gleason. © The Macmillan Co., N.Y., 1962. Pamphlet reprint, Paulist Press, 1963.

Contemporary Moral Theology, Vol. II: Marriage Questions, by John C. Ford, S.J. and Gerald Kelly, S.J. © The Newman Press, Westminster, Md., 1963.

Contraception and Catholics, by Louis Dupré. © Helicon Press, Baltimore, Md., 1964.

Family Planning and Modern Problems, by Stanislas de Lestapis, S.J. © Herder and Herder, New York, 1961.

Love and Control, by Léon Joseph Cardinal Suenens. © The Newman Press, Westminster, Md., 1961.

Marriage and Rhythm, by John L. Thomas, S.J. © The Newman Press, 1957.

The Problem of Population: Moral and Theological Considerations.

Edited by Donald N. Barrett. © University of Notre Dame Press, Notre Dame, Ind., 1964.

Sexual Relation in Christian Thought, by Derrick Sherwin Bailey. © Longmans, Green & Co. Ltd., England, 1958; © Harper, N.Y., 1959.

The Theology of Marriage, by Joseph E. Kerns, S.J. © Sheed and Ward, Inc., N.Y., 1964.

The Time Has Come, by John Rock, M.D. © Alfred A. Knopf, New York, 1963.

The author also acknowledges with appreciation the permission given by Mrs. Rosemary Ruether to use excerpts from her article, "A Catholic Mother Tells 'Why I Believe in Birth Control,'" published in *The Saturday Evening Post,* April 4, 1964; the copyright permission granted by that magazine to quote from "Letters," May 2, 1964; and the permission given by Msgr. George W. Casey, of St. Brigid's Church, Lexington, Mass., to quote at length from his article, "The Pastoral Crisis," printed in the June 5, 1964 issue of *Commonweal.*

Generous permissions for extensive quoting were received from *America,* the National Catholic Weekly Review published at 920 Broadway, N.Y.C.; *The Commonweal,* the layman's Catholic weekly, and from *Jubilee,* it being noted that the letters printed in the monthly's June, 1964 issue, from which representative excerpts were taken, will form part of a book, *Marriage, Love and Children,* to be published by the Dial Press.

The author is grateful for the friendly responses received from Msgr. S. Adamo, Executive Editor of the *Catholic Star Herald* of Camden, N.J.; and Robert G. Hoyt, Editor of *The National Catholic Reporter* of Kansas City, Mo., who, among other favors, approved the use of an excerpt from a copyrighted article by the Rev. Bernard Häring, C.Ss.R., printed May 29, 1964. To be thanked are still others who promptly answered queries; gave the author the benefit of their scholarship.

To the Rev. John L. Thomas, S.J., wise sociologist, the author owes the most profound debt of gratitude. He read the manuscript with the greatest care, noted mistakes, advised as to content and was unfailingly generous with his time.

For the confidence placed in a writer who is not a Catholic, the author respectfully thanks His Eminence Richard Cardinal Cushing; Msgr. Francis J. Lally, Editor of *The Pilot,* and the Rev. James A. O'Donohoe, Professor of Moral Theology at St. John's Seminary, Brighton, Mass., who was so kind as to read the manuscript.

For the conception of the work, she is first and last indebted to Winfield Best, Executive Vice-President of Planned Parenthood-World Population; and for many services rendered, to the organization's entire staff.

Contents

Foreword

We are living in exciting times. These are days when new light is being shed upon old concepts, days when those things which, in the past, had been accepted categorically and absolutely are now being re-examined more existentially in order to embrace the dimensions of the person. To my mind, it is a mistake to set aside these investigations without a hearing. In most instances they are being conducted, not that traditional doctrines might be undermined, but that their true worth might be made more apparent.

During the past few years, this process of reconsideration has been extended to the Church's teaching on the so-called birth control problem. This has been occasioned by modern philosophical, demographic, biological, and medical discoveries. Many in the Church are enthusiastic about these developments. They are delighted to see the Church opening herself up to the rich discoveries of modern science; they are encouraged that solutions which have been unthinkable in the past are being seriously offered by theologians for what is to many a heart-rending problem.

These sentiments, however, are not shared by everyone in the Church. Some good people are very disturbed by what they call the Church's "changing opinion" in the matter of birth control. It seems to me that this adverse reaction stems from two sources: 1) a failure to see the Church's teaching as a living, growing thing, the product of an organism which seizes upon every true scientific discovery in order to make the content of God's revelation better understood and more clearly formulated; 2) a failure to co-relate and study with an open mind all that is being written on this question by those who will admit that there is a problem and have the courage to discuss it openly and frankly.

If there is to be any "change" (I would prefer the word "refinement") in the traditional presentation of the Church's position on birth control, it is imperative that our people be prepared for it. To that end, it is necessary that they be acquainted with all the discussions that have been going on concerning the matter for the past few years. It is the particular genius of Mrs. Bromley's work to have done precisely this. She has presented clearly, accurately, and in an utterly unbiassed fashion an excellent summary of all the discussions on the doctrine of birth control which have marked the contemporary Catholic scene. Those who will take the time to read this book thoroughly can no longer plead ignorance of the present controversy. Those who will honestly and sincerely reflect upon the points of view which it presents cannot fail to appreciate the reality of the problem posed by the various authors cited and the logic of the solutions they present.

Catholic morality is of course a morality of principles. It is unfortunate, however, that it is often presented as something "cut and dried," unbending, and rigid. It is unfortunate, too, that papal statements which elaborate these principles are often quoted with little or no attempt to examine in detail the historical and scientific frame of reference within which they were written. Such approaches have ofen given the impression that our morality is a "morality of things" rather than a "morality of persons."

It should never be forgotten that although natural law does not change, our here-and-now interpretation and awareness of it does. It should not be forgotten either that the principles which Catholic morality sets forth are not to be applied in a vacuum but to real persons who live in real situations. When this is done within the framework which is essentially categoric but at the same time existentially Christian, the Church will no longer be seen as a heartless task-master, oblivious to the situations in which her people live. Instead, the Church will appear as the image of her Lord and founder who came to men in their own flesh, who made himself one with their problems, and who, even though He was their Lord, made himself their servant.

Richard Cardinal Cushing
Archbishop of Boston

August 1, 1964

Preface

Most of us are aware that past controversies relating to family planning have been marked more frequently by emotional intensity than clarity of thought. This should not surprise us. In the nature of things, concern with reproduction constitutes one of the major wellsprings of organization and individual motivation in all human societies. The initial challenge to cherished thought-ways in this regard probably requires something of a crusading spirit and this, in turn, invites defensive reactions.

Yet our past experiences have not been wholly useless. Basic issues are being clarified; traditional positions are being re-examined; and we have acquired some awareness that mature participation in a pluralist society, while it does not restrict our freedom to render witness to our personal commitments, requires the sincere cooperation of all in seeking acceptable solutions to problems involving the common good.

Among other things, such cooperation must be founded on mutual respect and the patient endeavor to understand opposing positions. For this reason the present study, sponsored by the Planned Parenthood Federation of America, merits special commendation. As they say in the schools, the author has done her homework well. Her task was not easy.

Although the normative values in the Catholic position regarding family regulation are relatively clear, the principles upon which they are based have been developed within a theological framework that is difficult to understand by one not trained in the scholastic tradition. All too often, terms like "nature," "end," "primary," "secondary," and so forth, become sources of confusion because Catholics and non-Catholics alike apparently forget that technical terms can be interpreted correctly only within their appropriate contexts. The author tends to by-pass this difficulty by quoting from approved sources, and though one sometimes feels that she is "content to quote where she cannot presently understand"—to turn a famous phrase of Burke's—her effort is admirable.

This study is not a treatise on Catholic marriage. It deals with some relevant aspects of the Catholic position as they presently appear in the current literature examined. If readers are surprised by the considerable divergence of views expressed by some of the writers cited, they should reflect that any rational moral judgment relating to a program of action in the practical order necessarily represents a conclusion based on the logical application of relevant premises of values to a set of pertinent facts.

Thus differences may develop over time either through increased understanding of the value-premises involved or because significant new factual evidence has come to light. Contemporary differences may also stem from several sources: in evaluating new situations individual thinkers may reach different conclusions concerning the implications of their moral principles; they may differ in their interpretations of the available facts; or they may display unequal awareness of the various factors that must be considered in formulating a balanced judgment. Examples of each of these sources of differences are presented in the text, suggesting that man's characteristic search for significance and meaning requires perennial rethinking of his current moral stance if he would "make sense" of his activities in a changing social context.

It has been said that men are generally right in what they stand for; it is in what they are against that they are most likely to err since they all too readily condemn what they do not understand. This work was conceived and carried out in the hope of fostering mutual understanding—may it be read in a similar spirit.

John L. Thomas, S.J.

Institute of Social Order
St. Louis University
June 25, 1964

Catholics and Birth Control

One | The Church's Historic Views
on Marriage and Human Sexuality

The Roman Catholic Church teaches today that conjugal love is a great good and that the procreation of children is not the sole purpose of marriage. As for the sex act itself when "two become one flesh" the Church teaches that in sacramental marriage, even if the act is performed at a time when procreation is impossible or unlikely, it symbolizes Christ's union with the Church and bears no taint of evil so long as illicit measures are not taken to prevent impregnation. This view of marital relations stands in contrast with the teaching of St. Augustine—strongly influential for many centuries—that the marital act, owing to the Fall of Adam and Eve, remains tainted with the evil of concupiscence.

In his famous encyclical, *Casti Connubii, Christian Marriage,* issued in 1930, Pope Pius XI declared that the laws "to strengthen and confirm and elevate" matrimony were made not by man but God and are therefore "immutable and inviolable." Pius XI accordingly cautioned:

> Since . . . the conjugal act is destined primarily by nature for the begetting of children, those who in exercising it deliberately frustrate its natural power and purpose, sin against nature and commit a deed which is shameful and intrinsically vicious.

But on the following page Pius XI noted:

> Nor are those considered as acting against nature who in the married state use their right in the proper manner although on account of natural reasons either of time or of certain defects, new life cannot be brought forth. For in matrimony as well as in the use of matrimonial rights there are also secondary ends, such as mutual aid, the cultivation of mutual love, and the quieting of concupiscence, which husband and wife are not forbidden to consider so long as they are subordinated to the primary end and so long as the intrinsic nature of the act is preserved.[1]

Pius XI thus put his stamp of approval on conclusions already reached by the Church's leading moral theologians of the 20th century. "Intercourse may honorably be sought . . . to show one's love," the Jesuit scholar Arthur Vermeersch had written in 1921.[2]

Pius XI's successor, Pius XII, specified, in 1951, the "medical, eugenical, social and economic indications * which make licit the observance of the non-fertile period [the practice of rhythm], at the same time reiterating Pius XI's teaching that to "deliberately frustrate" the conjugal act's "natural power and purpose" [by the practice of artificial birth control], is "to sin against nature." Later, in 1958, Pius XII declared the new progestin pill to be no less illicit if used as a direct contraceptive.†

---

* See p. 21.
† See p. 85.

In the years since then discussion within the Church concerning moral, and effective, methods of family limitation has increased at an accelerated pace. As a consequence, on June 23, 1964, Pope Paul VI announced, in an address to the cardinals of the Roman Curia, that "the matter is under study, a study as wide and deep as possible . . ." In a 5,000-word review of the first year of his pontificate, Paul VI noted "formidable problems" and "great events" of the future, and said, "We shall speak in conclusion of only one of these problems and of only one of these events which the future has in store for us."

> The problem—everyone talks about it—is that of so-called birth control, that is to say, of population increase on the one hand, and of family morality on the other. It is an extremely grave problem; it touches the sources of human life; it touches the sentiments and the interests which are closest to the experience of man and woman. It is an extremely complex and delicate problem.
>
> The Church recognizes its manifold aspects, that is to say, the manifold fields of competence, among which is certainly preeminent that of the spouses, of their liberty, of their conscience, of their love, of their duty.[3] *

Guarded as was Pope Paul's full pronouncement concerning the decision which will be reached as to how God's law is to be interpreted and taught, his recognition of "the liberty" and "the love" of married people, as well of their "conscience" and "duty," shows how far the Church has moved away from the centuries-old tradition which held even the conjugal act to be tainted with evil. That St. Augustine was largely responsible for the denigration of human sexuality which for so long pervaded the teaching of the Western Church, is one of the themes developed by the Belgian moral theologian, the Rev. Louis Janssens, in his monograph, "Morale Conjugale et

* For balance of Pope Paul's statement, see pp. 86-87.

Progestogenes." A member of the faculty of the Catholic University of Louvain, Father Janssens published his controversial, widely-discussed article in the fall of 1963 in the quarterly, *Ephemerides Theologicae Lovanienses.*

"Historical studies show," Father Janssens writes, "that the pessimistic and rigid ideas of the Stoics, Neo-Pythagoreans, Essenes and Gnostics on the conjugal act and sexual pleasure greatly influenced the thinking of many Church Fathers.* It was especially through the writing of St. Augustine that these tendencies passed into Western theology. . . ." [4]

The same point has been made by the Rev. Joseph Kerns, S.J., Chairman of Theology at Wheeling College, West Virginia. In a recent paper on "Relevant Currents in the History of Sexuality," Father Kerns notes:

> In the writings of Augustine and others who copied him for a thousand years we find, not marriage, but the sex instinct traced to original sin. Sexual intercourse is permitted between husband and wife only because the three assets of marriage, offspring, fidelity and the sacred pledge give it a distinctive quality which makes it morally good. [5]

In his book published in 1964, *The Theology of Marriage,* Father Kerns notes that the concept of sexual relations as evil

---

* The Anglican scholar, Derrick Sherwin Bailey, writes in his book, *Sexual Relations in Christian Thought:* "Stoicism . . . in its search for self-sufficiency and independence of earthly things, tended to reject matrimonial and domestic ties, while Neo-Pythagoreanism inclined towards a dualism which regarded coitus as a defilement and inculcated continence. Nor were these notions of sexual 'purity' characteristic only of Hellenistic asceticism, though they emerged from a Greek philosophical tradition at least as old as Orphism. They were echoed even from within the confines of Judaism in the teaching and practices of the Therapeutae and the Essenes; and a definite ascetical and dualistic strain can also be detected in the thought of Philo. . . . the Gnostics . . . ascribed wedlock and procreation to the malign intervention of the Demi-Urge." (pp. 5, 42) Dr. Bailey notes that the Church Fathers, in their view of sex, succumbed to the "oriental-hedonist dualism in which the age was steeped . . . even though dualism was condemned by the Church for its heretical influence in other directions." (p. 48)

goes back to Genesis, and thence to the pagan religions in and around the Holy Land.[6]

The concept can be traced, of course, to the view shared by all "primitive" peoples that sexuality is a sacred force and must consequently be subjected to numerous tabus and diverse regulations. Chastity or sexual continence is regarded as a means capable of increasing or concentrating the magico-religious force indispensable for obtaining a privileged religious status, as well as for success in activities which modern peoples would consider "profane." This view of sexuality as a sacred power existing in man and the Cosmos helps explain both the ritual promiscuity of the fertility cults, which so horrified the Jewish prophets, and the forbidding of sexual relations as being ritually unclean, during periods of religious initiation or before undertaking various enterprises.[7]

Since the serpent was looked upon throughout the Middle East as a sexual symbol, Father Kerns reasons, "Genesis may well be describing how woman's sexual attractiveness has ruined both man and herself, making men the slaves of a goddess and women the slaves of men." But he sees a difficulty with this interpretation, since "the serpent which the pagans associated with sex was a benign deity, whereas the Old Testament word for serpent is the same as that for a dragon and connotes an enemy of man.

"Scripture scholars will have to settle the question. The point of the story, that the evils of life are due to some rebellion against God, is the same in either interpretation . . . the author's [of Genesis] treatment of the sin itself is suggested more clearly in his description of its consequences":

> And the eyes of them both were opened: and when they perceived themselves to be naked, they sewed together fig leaves, and made themselves aprons. Gen. III, 7.

When God calls for the man:

> And he said: I heard thy voice in paradise; and I was afraid, because I was naked, and I hid myself. Gen. III, 10

"This certainly alters the impression," Father Kerns comments, "gained from the previous chapter." There the Biblical account reads:

> And they were both naked: to wit, Adam and his wife: and were not ashamed. Gen. II, 25

"It seems taken for granted," the Jesuit scholar continues, "that sexual intercourse is somehow incompatible with nearness to God. The Dead Sea Scrolls are evidence that, by the time of Christ, one Jewish sect was even encouraging its members not to marry. But these scattered texts must be read in a context that is especially clear whenever the Old Testament speaks of children." In the same Book of Exodus, Father Kerns explains, which has the people abstaining before their pact with God, marriage is so definitely expected of religious men that Yahweh is described as promising:

> There shall not be one fruitless nor barren in thy land: I will fill the number of thy days. Ex. XXIII, 26

The same theme—that it is a curse to live but not have children—Father Kerns points out, appears in "salvation histories, wisdom books, psalms." "The two discordant themes . . . an embarrassment at being male and female and a sense of impropriety in approaching God after sexual relations" are never reconciled.[8]

The Anglican scholar, Dr. Derrick Sherwin Bailey,* Chancellor of Wells Cathedral, writes in his book, *Sexual Relation in Christian Thought,*

> Among the Jews, marriage had always been held in relatively high esteem—not primarily (it must be admitted) for its traditional value, but because it was the means of propa-

---

* Formerly Study Secretary of the Moral Welfare Council of the Church of England.

gating the Holy People, of maintaining the institution of the family as the basis of society, and of assuring a shadowy semblance of immortality to a man in the offspring which he had begotten. Consequently the duty of early marriage was represented in rabbinical literature as incumbent upon every Hebrew male; for a man to remain single was . . . displeasing to God. Likewise, barrenness in a woman was a reproach hardly to be endured. . . . The Jewish attitude tended to induce a healthy, affirmative view of coitus which to some extent corrected an ingrained disposition to associate venereal acts and impulses with sin and evil. On the other hand, however, it did not affect the acceptance and perpetuation of a double standard of morality which was heavily weighted, as was usual in antiquity, on the side of the male . . .[9]

Augustine's view of marriage and of sex in marriage—a view that was to become the Christian view for many centuries —contrasts sharply with the Hebraic view. Agreeing with Fathers Janssens and Kerns as to Augustine's influence down through the years, Dr. Bailey writes:

Augustine must bear no small measure of responsibility for the insinuation into our culture of the idea, still widely current, that Christianity regards sexuality as something peculiarly tainted with evil.[10]

Born of a Christian mother in Numidia in 354 A.D., Augustine wrote as a skeptic and lived a licentious life until, at the age of 33 a mystical experience resulted in his conversion to Christianity. He became Bishop of Hippo in 395 and served there until his death in 430. The greatest of the Church Fathers, a philosopher whose works have been studied by men of all faiths, St. Augustine in his voluminous writings reverted again and again to marriage and the sexual impulse.

In *De bono conjugali,* Augustine wrote that since "procreation is the reason for marriage, it is the sole excuse for the conjugal act."[11] And in *Contra Faustum* he stressed that the eternal law which requires respect for the natural order, permits only those sexual relations which are necessary to procreation.[12]

Only then, the Bishop of Hippo held, is the sex act "licit and good." [13] Otherwise it becomes "a venial sin." [14]

In *De nuptiis et concupiscentia,* Augustine insisted that the sex act becomes "abominable debauchery" whenever an attempt is made to frustrate its natural consequences.[15] In the same work he wrote that wedded chastity transforms coitus from a satisfaction of lust to a necessary duty,[16] but that guilt is nevertheless transmitted from parents to children.[17]

In his teachings on marriage, St. Augustine leaned heavily on the practical advice which Paul gave married Christians in First Corinthians VII, 1-7. There the Apostle says:

> Now concerning the things whereof you wrote to me: It is good for a man not to touch a woman.
> But for fear of fornication, let every man have his own wife, and let every woman have her own husband.
> Let the husband render the debt to his wife, and the wife also in like manner to the husband.
> The wife hath not power of her own body, but the husband. And in like manner the husband also hath not power of his own body, but the wife.
> Defraud not one another, except, perhaps, by consent, for a time, that you may give yourselves to prayer; and return together again, lest Satan tempt you for your incontinency. But I speak this by indulgence, not by commandment.
> For I would that all men were even as myself: but everyone hath his proper gift from God; one after this manner, and another after that.

"In this passage," Father Janssens observes, "St. Paul justifies marriage and sexual relations on grounds other than procreation . . . Yet St. Augustine manages to explain the Apostle's affirmations without abandoning his own principles." Augustine interpreted Paul's injunction with regard to conjugal rights to mean that "it is the duty of a married person to respond to the demand of the partner to save the latter from adultery." [18]

So as to reconcile this passage with his own view that it is a venial sin for a married person to demand the conjugal act for any reason other than procreation, Augustine held that Paul, in Verse 7, offered "pardon" to couples who "return together" to avoid temptation.[19] Whether the Greek word used by Paul, translated as "indulgence" in the *Douay* version quoted above, meant "pardon," implying venial sin, or merely "permission" was to be debated for many centuries.

Continence, Augustine insisted, should be practiced whenever conception is not possible, as for example during a wife's pregnancy or after the menopause.[20] "It goes without saying," Father Janssens observes, "that St. Augustine would have condemned the practice of periodic continence . . . Indeed he severely criticized the Manicheans, who advised their followers to avoid conception by abstaining from intercourse during periods when conception was possible."[21] [22]

More concerned with sexual purity than with procreation, Augustine went so far as to commend total abstinence to the married, saying "the sooner husband and wife abstain by mutual consent, the better." [23] "We know many of our brethren . . ." Augustine recorded, "who in the name of Christ practice an entire restraint . . ." [24] But some couples of the time, like Jerome's correspondent Rustica, proved unequal to the rigors of asceticism.[25]

Ambivalent in his attitude, Augustine reproached those heretics who advised married folk to avoid procreation, and charged them with condemning "marriage by removing its purpose." [26] He pointed out that the word "matrimonium" derives from the word "maternity." [27] And he read into Genesis II, 18—"It is not good for man to be alone; let us make him a helpmeet unto himself"—his own meaning that God gave woman to man only for purposes of procreation.[28]

In his various writings, Father Janssens notes, Augustine found Christian marriage intrinsically good because of its three benefits: *proles, fides, sacramentum.*[29]

Biblical authority for the first good, *proles,* was found by Augustine not only in Genesis I, 28—"And God blessed them, saying: "Increase and multiply . . ."—but also in First Timothy, V. 14, where Paul says, "I will therefore that the younger should marry, bear children, be mistresses of families . . ."

Marital fidelity, *fides,* Augustine held, was enjoined by the Apostle in First Corinthians, VII, 4, where Paul speaks of the husband's power over his wife's body and of hers over his. This verse Augustine read to mean that a Christian married person must save the partner from adultery for the latter's sake,[30] and not for his or her own sake, through reasons of jealousy, a motive condoned by the pagans.

In view of the third good, *sacramentum,* Augustine held that for a man to send away a wife who is sterile and marry another was forbidden by the law which Christ proclaimed in Matthew XIX, 6,—"What therefore God hath joined together, let no man put asunder"; also by Paul's saying to the Ephesians, in V, 31-32, "For this cause shall a man leave his father and mother, and shall be joined unto his wife, and they two shall be one flesh. This is a great sacrament; but I speak in Christ and in the Church." It is through this holy sacrament, this third good, Augustine declared, that Christian marriage is glorified, as compared with marriage among all other peoples, who recognize only the first two goods.[31]

The conjugal charity—or love—which Paul invokes in Ephesians V, 25—"Husbands, love your wives, as Christ also loved the Church, and delivered himself up for it"—was viewed by the Bishop of Hippo as a purely spiritual love based on a union of souls and not on carnal relations or on the *libido.*[32] This concept, Father Janssens comments, lies "at the very heart of the dualism which St. Augustine introduced into conjugal life." It was a concept which prevented him "from seeing that sexual intercourse could have a positive significance in sacramental marriage." [33]

Father Kerns for his part, points out that the dualistic view of marriage held by St. Augustine as well as other Church Fathers, with its built-in doctrine that marriage, though not in itself sinful was the result of original sin, ran counter to scripture. "The episode at Cana," he writes, "was symbolic. Like the Father in the Old Testament, so Christ in the New presents himself as the founder of marriage. . . ." [34]

Analysing the dilemma in which the Fathers found themselves, Dr. Bailey, the Anglican, writes: "They were compelled by the Church's tenacious and reverential belief in the beneficent Creator-God of the Old Testament to affirm the essential goodness of all his works; yet cultural and temperamental factors inhibited them from treating marriage and sexuality in the positive spirit of Jewish naturalism." He continues:

> From the impending dilemma, however, the Pauline double ethical standard offered a way of escape; by ranking the single above the wedded state it permitted the Fathers to acknowledge the divine institution and the practical utility of marriage while at the same time subordinating it as a lesser good to virginity and widowhood. . . . [35]

To support their position the early Christian writers, Dr. Bailey explains, argued that "the advent of Christ had modified God's original intention in creating male and female." "Under the old covenant, they contended, marriage and coitus were necessary . . . in order to insure the increase of the Lord's people, and the establishment and continuance of a line from which the Messiah might arise. . . . With the arrival of a new dispensation, however, carnal propagation ceased to be obligatory and salvation became dependent, not upon generation but regeneration . . . it was a time not to embrace but to refrain from embracing. Indeed, if all would abstain, the City of God would be filled the more speedily, and the end of the world hastened." [36] [37]

Augustine's rigorous views on human sexuality were the fruit, Dr. Bailey suggests, not only of the age he lived in, but of his own licentious life prior to his conversion, as reflected in his *Confessions*. Plagued in his earlier years by religious and philosophical doubts, Augustine prayed to God again and again, "Give me chastity—but not yet." [38] [39]

Particularly offensive and embarrassing to Augustine was the act of coitus, Dr. Bailey writes,[40] "with its uncontrollable orgasm." "He blushed to think that even the good work of generation cannot be accomplished without 'a certain amount of bestial movement.' [41] He believed that . . . the shameful copulations which men and women endure in the discharge of their procreative functions are not natural to our kind, but result from the transgressions of our first parents. In Paradise, Augustine maintained, Adam and Eve were naked and unashamed because their genitals . . . were wholly under control and obedient to the dictates of their wills [42] . . . They did not venture upon coitus before their expulsion from Eden, but had they done so, their congress would have been without lascivious heat or unseemly passion." [43] [44]

"Had the Fathers and Schoolmen," the Anglican scholar observes, "understood the physiology and the psychology of venereal intercourse, and the neural mechanisms by which the orgasm is caused, they could never have concluded that coitus is an evil or sinful act. . . . In other words, they were unaware that the phenomena which they attributed to the effect of the Fall were actually ordained by God as part of the normal operation of the human body; and that coitus in Paradise, as they conceived it, was not only unnatural but also impossible." [45]

About a century and a half after the death of the Bishop of Hippo, Pope Gregory I slightly modified Augustine's theory of human sexuality, holding that the evil element in coitus is not in the act itself, nor in the urge which leads to coition but in the peculiar sensual pleasure enjoyed at the time of the act.[46]

The dualism which, in the words of Father Janssens, "erected a barrier between the sexual life of husband and wife, and their union based on spiritual love," was carried over into the Mediaeval Church.[47] In the 12th century Hugh of St. Victor held that only spiritual union—such a relationship as existed between the Blessed Virgin and St. Joseph—was essential to marriage.[48] Yet in the same century Pope Alexander III held that coitus alone could render a marriage indissoluble—questions of divorce and remarriage being of great concern to the Mediaeval Church.[49]

Through the Dark Ages and the Middle Ages, Father Kerns points out, "married couples were completely unaware of what theologians were writing [in Latin] about the sex instinct and original sin"—even though they had heard about Adam and Eve. "Most of them actually could not read. Saxon villagers and recently converted Lombards knew little more of Augustine than his name. . . . Without any special thought on the matter, they married and then made use of their marriage rights. And no one told them they were wrong. They cannot be compared with Catholics today who practice contraceptive birth control. . . ."[50]

In the 13th century, the age of the Great Scholastics, St. Thomas Aquinas adhered, with a few modifications, to St. Augustine's view that human sexuality is inherently sinful. While the Angelic Doctor found the sex act meritorious when performed by married persons in a state of grace, either to discharge the marital debt or to procreate children, he also held that neither of these ends relieved coition of its intrinsic taint of evil.[51] Just as Augustine had been influenced by Platonic dualism, Aquinas and his fellow Scholastics followed Aristotle's doctrine of the "golden mean,"—the rule of reason over the passions.[52] Dr. Bailey explains:

Aquinas located the seat of coital evil, not in the sex act itself, nor in concupiscence, nor yet in venereal pleasure, but in what he regarded as the inevitable irrationality of the *copula* in fallen humanity; but for this defect husband and wife could not be held morally responsible—it was simply a punishment which had come to rest upon the race in consequence of its initial rebellion against the Creator.[53]

Aquinas also followed Augustine in holding that woman was indispensable to man only as the conceiver of his children, since, Aquinas wrote, a husband in his other activities can be helped more effectively by another man.[54]

As had Augustine, Aquinas found prostitution a necessary evil. The former, after deploring the sordidness of harlotry, had written, "Yet remove prostitutes from human affairs, and you will pollute all things with lust . . ."; [55] and at another point had said that "the earthly city has made the use of harlots a lawful immorality." [56] Aquinas wrote that "God allows certain evils to exist in the world, which he might prevent, lest greater evils ensue;" and that likewise "in human government . . . those who are in authority rightly tolerate certain evils, lest certain goods be lost or certain greater evils be incurred." [57]

Aquinas' views, like Augustine's, lived long after him. Dr. Bailey points out that as late as the 15th century, the gentle humanist, John Colet, reflected Augustine's views in the lectures he gave at the University of Oxford. Colet taught that although marriage was originally useful for generation, it had lost this justification and was merely a concession to human weakness.[58]

The Council of Trent, which met from 1545 to 1563 during the Counter Reformation, as the first true ecumenical council, codified the Church's views on marriage. It dealt with the institution, Father Janssens writes, without regard to the exercise of the marital right. "It considered only the community of life and love which is the essence of sacramental marriage," and "described the properties of marriage, as indissolubility, unity, the love of the spouses. It underscored that Grace, which Christ merited for us by His passion, perfects natural love, confirms the indissoluble unity, and sanctifies the spouses. . . ." [59]

The Roman Catechism, prepared at the direction of the Council of Trent as an aid to the clergy in their instruction of the laity, "reiterated," Father Janssens notes, "this double fashion of considering marriage, declaring that the first reason (*prima causa*) why a man and woman should marry is to enjoy a community of life and love, and the second reason (*altera causa*) is to have children." [60] *

But it should be noted, Father Kerns observes, that Charles V's theologian at Trent, Dominic Soto, wrote:

> Nature has wisely attached pleasure to that act because of the need to conserve the race. . . . Therefore just as taking one's food and drink with pleasure is no sin, neither is marital intercourse. . . . And certainly those who say the contrary, in other words, that it is a sin unless a man abhors the pleasure involved, are trying to deprive men of their natural feeling. The mind is simply not able to elicit displeasure in that situation. [61]

Father Janssens finds it significant that not until the middle of the 17th century could a leading theologian write that it had by then become accepted doctrine to interpret St. Paul's phrase to mean "permission" and not "pardon." That is to say, married couples, in coming together again, so as to avoid the sin of adultery, as after a fast, were not held to be committing a venial sin, as Augustine had insisted. [62]

* The Catechism of the Council of Trent, in setting forth "the reasons because of which man and woman ought to be joined in marriage" states clearly: "The first is precisely the companionship sought by the natural instinct of different sex, and brought about in the hope of mutual aid, so that each may help the other to bear more easily the troubles of life, and to support the weakness of old age. The second is the desire to have children." (*Catechism of the Council of Trent, II, 8, 13.*)

Evolution in the Church's viewpoint came gradually. In the late 18th century, Father Kerns tells us, Jean Grou wrote that for a married couple to have relations to foster their love for each other is "not alien to the use of marriage." [63]

By the beginning of the 20th century, Father Janssens notes, "the moralists were finally agreed that a moderate seeking of pleasure though conjugal relations is not morally wrong." But in some of the arguments supporting this position he finds vestiges of the old dualism.[64]

"Today's marriage manuals," the Belgian moralist writes, "certainly do not fail to mention the inter-dependence between sexual intercourse and mutual love of husband and wife. But . . . they do not go deeply enough . . ." He points out that Pius XII did go deeply into the implications of marital intercourse when he explained why artificial insemination, even between husband and wife for reasons of procreation, is morally illicit.[65] Speaking to the Italian midwives in 1951, Pius XII declared:

> The marital act, in its natural structure, is a personal action, a simultaneous and direct cooperation of husband and wife which, because of the very nature of the agents and the distinctive character of the act is the expression of the mutual self-giving that, in the words of Scripture, makes them "one flesh." [66]

"The body is the mediator of love," Father Janssens himself writes, noting that only man among all living species can attain such an act of union. Conjugal love, in his words, "is a communion . . . in which two persons give themselves one to the other, as husband and wife, positively and exclusively— since "the corporeal self, man's very being, is indivisible." When marital coition "really inspires love," the husband will wish the happiness of his wife and she, his. "One should not seek sexual pleasure for oneself, in an egoistic fashion . . . one gives and one receives in giving." Conjugal love rules out "all egoism, all hedonism." If the act which expresses this love to the full is engaged in at a time when procreation is possible, it seeks to incarnate life, Father Janssens explains.[67]

From the viewpoint of an American Jesuit, Father Kerns describes conjugal love in the same positive terms as does the Belgian moralist, but with a slightly different emphasis. He notes that "the change in what Christian writers said from the second till the 20th century reflects nothing so much as a struggle between two cultural views on human sexuality, with the Christian view gradually prevailing." Father Kerns continues:

> This Christian view discloses certain truths about human life as Christ reveals it. First, the tendency that each of us feels to make himself the axis around which the rest of the world revolves, to use other men and even God to his own advantage, is the result of a primal sin which has made us inheritors of a damaged human nature. But though sexual intercourse is one occasion when that unruly tendency displays itself, the sex instinct is not the result of original sin. Much less is it the continuation of rebellion. Both the instinct and its expression in marriage are features of human life as God designed it.[68]

"The rigorist," the Jesuit scholar adds, "errs as badly as the libertine when he describes the intercourse of husband and wife in terms of physical pleasure. That particular activity of a human being is supposed to say something. It is essentially a gesture. Just as words are designed to convey thought, this gesture has been devised by the Creator as the expression of a unique attitude toward another human being. As real and essential as the connection with life is its connection with love."

Two | Responsible Parenthood

It is a mistake to assume that only the large Catholic family is the good Catholic family in the eyes of the Church. Certainly in all of its teachings the Roman Catholic Church attaches great merit to couples who are fruitful and multiply. But modern Catholic writers are stressing that Canon 1013—one of those Church regulations which members are duty-bound to obey—defines the primary purpose of marriage as "the procreation *and education* of children." (italics added)

To educate a child, these writers point out, means to rear him in an environment conducive to his physical, mental and spiritual growth. Foresight may, therefore, be required of parents in the spacing or limiting of the number of their children. That this may morally be done by recourse to the natural or rhythm method of birth prevention has been for some time accepted Catholic teaching.

As early as 1930 Pope Pius XI made it clear in his encyclical, *Casti Connubii, On Christian Marriage,* that those are not "considered as acting against nature who in the married state use their right in the proper manner although on account of natural reasons either of time or of certain defects, new life cannot be brought forth." *

Two decades passed. The Vatican became increasingly aware of the problems of poverty and of the findings of medical scientists and eugenicists. On Oct. 29, 1951, Pius XII addressed the Italian midwives on "Moral Questions Affecting Married Life." One part of this important allocution was to form the basis for an emerging Catholic concept of responsible parenthood.

In the course of this address Pius XII re-emphasized "the value and inviolability of human life;" spoke at length of "the greatness and joy of motherhood" and stressed that upon married couples "nature and the Creator impose the function of helping the conservation of the human race." [1] But he also noted the problem which

> presents itself today whether and how far the obligation of being ready in the service of motherhood is consistent with the increasingly common use of the naturally sterile periods . . .[2]

Addressing himself to this "serious" question, Pius XII continued:

> From the obligation of making this positive contribution it is possible to be exempt, for a long time and even for the whole duration of married life, if there are serious reasons, such as those often provided in the so-called "indications" of the medical, eugenical, economic and social order. It therefore follows that the observance of the infertile periods may be licit from the moral point of view; and under the conditions mentioned it is so in fact. Nevertheless, in the

* See p. 4.

absence—according to a reasonable and equitable judgment
—in the absence of similar serious reasons, whether personal
or circumstantial, the intention of married people to avoid
habitually the fecundity of their union, while continuing to
give full satisfaction to their sensual desires, can be based
only a false outlook on life or on motives that are foreign
to true ethical standards.[3]

A month later Pius XII returned to the same theme, in an
address before the National Congress of the Family Front.
While he deplored the growing "subversion of conjugal
morality" and heaped praise on parents who courageously rear
large families, Pius XII said the family must be preserved
from

the degrading bondage to which it is reduced by that mentality which tends to make of it a mere organism at the
service of the social community, for the purpose of pro-
creating a sufficient mass of "human material." [4]

After referring to the effects of two world wars, to the
housing crisis and the unemployment problem, Pius XII
declared:

. . . the Church knows how to consider with sympathy and
understanding the real difficulties of the married state in
our day. Therefore, in our last allocution on conjugal morality, we affirmed the legitimacy and, at the same time, the
limits—in truth very wide—of a regulation of offspring
which, unlike so-called "birth control," is compatible with
the law of God. One may even hope (but in this matter the
Church naturally leaves the judgment to medical science)
that science will succeed in providing this licit method with
a sufficiently secure basis. The most recent information
seems to confirm such a hope.[5]

Christian couples have a responsibility they did not have,
an eminent cleric has observed, before Ogino and Knaus in-
dependently published in 1930 their findings on the fertile

and sterile days of a woman's menstrual cycle. The Archbishop of Malines-Brussels, His Eminence Léon Joseph Cardinal Suenens, one of four Cardinals appointed by Pope Paul VI to the Steering Committee of the Ecumenical Council, writes in his book, *Love and Control:*

> What used to be left to chance was now put under men's control. After a fashion it put the key to the kingdom of life in men's hands, in most cases at least. Also, while the old choice used to be either indeterminable fertility or complete abstention, there now arose a new problem of conscience: the voluntary use of the periods of fertility and sterility. . . .

"Prudence . . ." Cardinal Suenens writes, "means choosing from the entirety of complex reality what is most in line with God's whole plan for us. . . ."

> It is worthy of a Christian to perform an act of such staggering natural and supernatural consequence in complete consciousness of the act's cause. Bringing a child into the world is a sacred act; it is fitting that a couple should decide upon it once they have previously considered it before God and deliberately determined to do it, leaving nothing to chance. The expected and hoped-for child will be greeted by more love to help him develop the more his home was prepared for his arrival. This reflection, surrounded as it is by prayer, dynamized by the theological virtues and inspired by filial confidence in God, will then be an act of homage to God . . . Reflection and prayer are the exact opposite of egoistic self-concern. . . .[6]

The role that science has played in enabling man to exert a controlling influence over procreation has also been alluded to by a Dutch clerical leader, Msgr. W. Bekkers, Bishop of 's-Hertogenbosch. Speaking on March 21, 1963 on a discussion program conducted by the Catholic Broadcasting Station in the Netherlands, Bishop Bekkers said in part:

. . . birth regulation—which is, incidentally, something quite distinct from birth control—is becoming an integral part of the total task entrusted to married people. It means that man has got to project the number of his offspring against the whole, kaleidoscopic background of his married life; there is no particular merit merely in having a large or a small family.[7]

That there is a need "to purify the concept of responsible parenthood" has been stressed by the Rev. Bernard Häring, C.Ss.R., recognized as one of the Church's leading moral theologians. In a colloquy at the University of Notre Dame, held in the late summer of 1963, Father Häring, a consultant to the Theological Commission of the Ecumenical Council, explained:

Responsible parenthood in view of Catholic morality means giving a generous response to the challenging appeal of the gifts of God. Nobody can make this act of judgment as to what responsibility means for them other than married couples themselves, in consideration of all the factors of their lives, especially health, home conditions and educational facilities.

Father Häring stresses that a couple should not decide "once and forever" the number of children they wish to have, but should "remain open to the challenge of a new situation." "Responsible parenthood," he points out, "can mean for one family not to desire more than one child. It can mean for another to desire, even after the tenth child, one more. The judgment of responsibility is necessarily also an authentic image of the religious and moral life of those who make it."[8]

Elaborating this concept, in the June 5, 1964 issue of *Commonweal*, Father Häring writes:

Just as the first conjugal "knowing" is only the beginning of an ever deepening dialogue of love between the spouses, so their attention to God's will and their readiness and capacity to make of everything a response of faith, of hope and of love must gradually attain new dimensions. Any rigid calculating and planning for the entire future must be recognized as the arch-enemy of progressive maturity.[9]

At the same time, the German theologian calls attention to the 20th century context in which a couple must make their "response of faith, of hope and of love." "In earlier times," Father Häring said at Notre Dame, "children were an essential goal for the economic and social needs of the family. The assurance for old age and the function of the family as a unit of production made it desirable to have many children. Furthermore, there was no medical diagnosis as to the dangers of a new pregnancy. Infant mortality was generally more than 50 to 60 per cent. The problems of education in a static society were not too complicated. All this has changed. In many cases it would be catastrophic for a young family to have four children in the first four years. The health of the mother would be totally exhausted, the financial situation desperate, and so on. Not a lack of generosity but rather a sense of responsibility and realism imposes on the young couple the necessity of spacing pregnancies from the very beginning. This is necessary even if they wish a large family under good conditions."[10]

As for the views of leading moral theologians in this country, the Rev. John C. Ford, S.J., of the Catholic University of America, and the late Rev. Gerald Kelly, S.J., of St. Mary's College in Kansas, note in their book, *Marriage Questions*, that "the discovery of the sterile period" has confronted a great many Catholics with a "new and basic question." Each married couple must now decide "what are the respective roles of divine providence and human providence in the planning of their families?" "It is a basic question," they continue, "because it involves decisions as to how in the concrete circumstances of their lives they can best fulfill their twofold vocation, a vocation both to parenthood and to conjugal love.

The sphere of human providence has clearly been widened. . . .

> Given a situation where the number of children is a serious practical problem, if there exists a legitimate, effective, and reasonably available method of regulating the size of the family, Christian prudence requires that this method must be taken into consideration along with other factors . . .

"Man's reason," the two Jesuit authors continue, "makes him share in divine providence in a special way. When reason makes new discoveries of a morally acceptable kind, he must use his reason to plan his life accordingly. . . ." They recall that St. Thomas Aquinas wrote: "Among all others, the rational creature is subject to divine providence in a certain more excellent way, *insofar as he partakes of a share of providence by being provident both for himself and others.*"

Fathers Ford and Kelly observe that "this is the pastoral problem about which more and more Catholics are consulting spiritual advisors and confessors today." "It cannot be solved," they comment, "by disparaging periodic continence, and piously reminding the faithful that God will provide. They may be all too well aware that they themselves cannot provide, and that when the next child comes it will be a relative or a public agency that will have to provide. Nor can it be solved by a casuistry of sin. . . . The problem is to arrive at a practical judgment as to when reliance on divine providence should be supplemented by the exercise of human providence."

The two Jesuit moral theologians observe further that "a thoroughly Catholic notion of responsible parenthood includes the fostering of religious and priestly vocations, the training of children so that they will not marry before they are sufficiently mature and otherwise prepared for the vocation of marriage, and sufficient spacing of children so that they can be reared according to reasonably adequate religious and cultural standards." [11]

Writing on the same theme, the St. Louis University sociologist, the Rev. John L. Thomas, S.J. stresses in his book, *Marriage and Rhythm,* that those who choose marriage should seek perfection "by being good husbands and wives, good fathers and mothers." But he notes that there has been "confusion" among Catholics concerning Pius XII's four categories of "indications" justifying the regulation of offspring. "There are those," Father Thomas comments, "who apparently maintain that a valid reason exists only if a future pregnancy would seriously threaten the life of the mother. This is clearly not the mind of the Pope." [12]

In his elaboration of Pius XII's "indications," Father Thomas groups under "medical" such conditions as: 1. The father psychically unable to stand the strain of rearing a numerous family. 2. Pregnancy involving unusual organic difficulties for the mother. 3. The mother's state of health poor. 4. The wife unable to carry a pregnancy to term. 5. The mother subject to "unusual strain in rearing children." 6. Prolonged sickness among the children or a defective child.

As to problems of bad heredity, Father Thomas notes that a couple who have given birth to a deformed or defective child, will "justly want to know whether their next child will possess the same traits." He advises consultation with a specialist.

Some of the principal "adverse economic factors" as listed by the author are: 1. Unemployment or physical disability of the father. 2. Father's lack of vocational training or parents' inability to manage well. 3. Debt due to accidents, sickness, hospital and doctor bills. 4. Probable future cost of educating their children in accordance with Christian standards.

On economic factors in general, Father Thomas writes:

What is involved . . . is a comparison between the good of the family—the good of husband and wife and the children already born—and the good of a possible future child. Experience shows that sincere Christian couples tend to make responsible decisions in this regard . . .

The social system, Father Thomas comments, sometimes creates conditions which make "family life unusually difficult." He refers to:

1. The crisis created by modern war.
2. Trend of early marriage among young men who are completing their studies so as adequately to fulfill their role as breadwinners. But, the author cautions, only "under serious pressure should a young couple consider postponing for a time this profoundly unifying experience of marriage" [i.e. parenthood].
3. Lack of housing affording "reasonable privacy and a proper environment."
4. "Living-in" with relatives.
5. No aid available to mother in supervision of small children in urban environment.

In summary, Father Thomas observes:

> The family is a human institution. It is composed of concrete individuals, characterized by their varied abilities and limitations. . . . Although all couples bring a dedication of themselves to marriage, each couple will differ in their capacity to fulfill its primary purpose. . . .[13]

Reflecting the "confusion" among Catholics regarding their duty to procreate, to which Father Thomas earlier referred, a poll of teen-agers was reported in 1961 in the *Catholic Family Leader,* the news bulletin of the National Catholic Welfare Conference. In a news item captioned "Marriage Duty Clarification," Msgr. John A. Goodwine, a moral theologian of Mamaroneck, N.Y., was quoted as having found that a majority of high-school seniors whom he had questioned over a three- to four-year period, believed that married couples are duty-bound to have as many children as possible, and that family planning is absolutely forbidden by the moral law.

While Msgr. Goodwine made it clear that marriage prepera-
tion courses given by priests should present "the Christian
ideal of fertility and parenthood," he was quoted as having
said:

> It would not seem out of place to acknowledge that the
> marriage act is a human act and, as such, is to be exercised
> in a reasonable manner. . . .[14]

"The new possibility of larger surviving families occasions
problems," the Rev. William J. Gibbons, S.J., sociologist and
demographer of Fordham University, writes. After stressing
that "modern man is not permitted to do anything contrary
to the purposes for which God created sex and marriage," he
continues:

> If there is no regulation of offspring whatsoever, will par-
> ents be able to provide adequate education for their chil-
> dren? Will others be able to do so if the parents cannot?
> Education means something more than formal schooling.
> As Canon Law puts it . . . it means rearing in the full sense
> of the word. This includes spiritual formation, necessities
> of life, guidance and protection until adulthood.[15]

"In this country," an editorial, "Women and Rhythm," in
the March 8, 1963 issue of *Commonweal* read, "the rapid
drop in the average age at which men and women marry now
means that a woman can easily bear four or five children by
the age of thirty—and still have anywhere from ten to 15 fertile
years left. At the same time, the rising cost of housing, the
trend toward smaller houses, and the cost of education now
make the raising of very large families increasingly difficult.
These facts are easily noticeable—and it is both unfair and
unrealistic to assume that those who, in their personal lives,
find them a heavy burden are necessarily weak in their de-
votion to Catholic family ideals. . . ."

Commonweal is the country's only Catholic weekly edited

by laymen. The editors in their remarks noted "still another change, possibly the one least considered by most Catholics":

> It is now taken for granted, among Catholics and non-Catholics alike, that women have many talents to contribute to society—talents other than those of child-bearing and child-rearing. Women also have minds; they are increasingly being trained to use them. In the past it was assumed that woman's proper role was intrinsically the "hidden" role; like other minority groups throughout history, women were told to be passive, humble, meek and self-effacing . . . But who can sanely sustain such a myth any longer? Today, women are effectively demonstrating that they can do remarkably well in many of those "active" roles once thought appropriate only for men. The consequences of this change are immense. . . .

It is not generally known that a Catholic couple who as responsible parents wish to space or limit the number of their children, may do so without consulting a priest. In his *Catholic Marriage Manual,* Msgr. George A. Kelly, Director of the Family Life Bureau of the Archdiocese of New York, makes this point clear, but first says: "All available evidence proves what we know from personal experience that large families—those of five or more children—are generally happier than small families. They are better for parents, better for the children, better for society." [16] As to the Church's teaching, Msgr. Kelly writes:

> The Church neither approves nor disapproves *per se* restricting marital intercourse to the safe period. If a man and wife . . . meet the proper conditions, the Church finds no objection, since the marital act is performed as God designed it. The couple so deciding, presuming the honesty of their motives, do not need the permission of the priest before they begin its practice. While they may wish to consult a priest about the morality involved, the basic decision

to have four rather than six children belongs to the couple themselves. . . .

In his interpretation of Pius XII's "medical indications," Msgr. Kelly advises any wife who is told by a physician that another pregnancy might be fatal, to consult an obstetrician in a Catholic hospital. With regard to "economic indications," he writes:

> The obligation of parenthood does not require a couple to have as many children as is humanly possible, as some critics allege. However, they should have as many children as they can support reasonably. This does not mean that they should be deeply in debt to the loan companies before practising periodic continence. Nor does it mean that rhythm is justified until they have sufficient savings to insure a college education for the child.

Young couples who have not yet had a child are counselled by Msgr. Kelly not to use rhythm during a period when emotional needs are great and they have not yet learned whether they are fertile.

Under "social indications," Father Kelly refers to "poor housing conditions" which he, as a New Yorker, especially understands. These, he says, "may force a couple to live in such crowded quarters that an additional child would create a great burden." [17]

In an article on responsible parenthood published in *America* in 1962, Msgr. Kelly cautioned against "a secularist philosophy" which leads to "a stingy approach to child-bearing." In this connection, he wrote:

> All too often, in our culture, conscientious fathers and mothers are being led to feel that they must give their children every comfort, when another brother or sister might be the best thing for them. . . .[18]

While stressing that motives for limiting or spacing children must be truly moral, a number of Catholic leaders and teachers have thought it important to make the Church's position on responsible parenthood unmistakably clear.

Recently Richard Cardinal Cushing, Archbishop of Boston, in referring to "the much misunderstood Catholic position," wrote:

> the Church is not opposed to birth control as such but to the use of artificial means to control births.[19]

The Rev. John A. O'Brien, Research Professor of Theology at the University of Notre Dame, has told readers of *Look:*

> Instead of Catholics' being obliged or even encouraged to beget the greatest possible number of offspring, as many non-Catholics imagine, the ideal of responsible parenthood is stressed, so that parents will be able to provide properly for their offspring.[20]

From Europe comes an important book entitled *Family Planning and Modern Problems,* by the Rev. Stanislas de Lestapis, S.J., a noted family sociologist at the *Institut Catholique* in Paris. Father de Lestapis was the Holy See's representative to the United Nations World Population Conference in Rome in 1954. With relation to family size, he writes:

> Every couple owes it . . . to God, the creator of human love and sexuality, to itself, to the community, to procreate those children whom it will be able to bring up and to prepare adequately for life. There is an optimum number for each family and each family alone can judge what it is. Both the temporal and spiritual values must be taken into account . . . and a way be found to keep the right balance between them. . . .

On the question of whether the Church *approves* of birth regulation, the Paris priest goes further than New York's Msgr. Kelly. Father de Lestapis declares:

> . . . the Catholic Church, faced with the possibility of birth limitation, teaches that there is, in principle, a right, or better, a duty, to practice a form of birth regulation based on careful thought, provided that this regulation is inspired solely by motives of genuine charity, and that it respects the order of values inherent in the sexual function and also the pattern of its structural factors.[21]

In a philosophical comment on marriage, Father de Lestapis writes:

> We cannot insist too much on the fact that divine love, by entrusting its own great designs to human love, gives to the latter its genuine dimensions. And the converse is true . . . the true home should be able through its integrating power daily to enlarge the inner consciousness of man, tempted as he is always to be wholly absorbed in external activities.[22]

Three | The Natural Law and the Purposes of Marriage

Why, many non-Catholics ask, does the Church condemn "artificial contraception" as immoral, while it finds licit under prescribed circumstances the use of the rhythm method? The end sought—prevention of pregnancy—is the same, no matter what method is used.

To understand why the Catholic Church makes a sharp distinction between methods it is necessary to understand its teaching on the natural law and the purposes of marriage.

Pius XI, it will be recalled, declared that the primary end of marriage—"procreation and education of offspring," is not to be subordinated to its secondary ends—"mutual aid, the cultivation of mutual love and the quieting of concupiscence." *

But Pius XI also declared in *Casti Connubii*:

> This mutual inward moulding of husband and wife, this determined effort to perfect each other, can in a very real

* See p. 4.

sense, as the *Roman Catechism* teaches, be said to be the
chief reason and purpose of matrimony, provided matrimony be looked at not in the restricted sense as instituted
for the proper conception and education of the child, but
more widely as the blending of life as a whole and the
mutual interchange and sharing thereof."

On their side, most of the Protestant churches make no
distinction between the ends of—or spiritual benefits to be
derived from—marriage. The National Council of Churches'
statement on the subject speaks of "the fundamentally
spiritual character of the basic purpose of marriage, which
can be served through parenthood, companionship and vocation." In the matter of contraception, the Council asserts that
"motives rather than methods form the primary moral
issue." [2] * Among all but Orthodox Jews the position is very
much the same. The Rabbinical Alliance states that "Orthodox Judaism does not condone any artificial birth control

---

* In 1930 the Lambeth Conference, attended by 260 Bishops of the
Anglican Church, reversed that Church's traditional condemnation of the
practice of birth control. Its Declaration of 1930 reads in part: "Where
there is a clearly felt moral obligation to limit or avoid parenthood, the
method must be decided on Christian principles. The primary and obvious
method is complete abstinence from intercourse (as far as may be necessary) in a life of discipline and self-control lived in the power of the
Holy Spirit. Nevertheless in those cases where there is . . . a clearly felt
moral obligation . . . and where there is a morally sound reason for
avoiding complete abstinence, the Conference agrees that other methods
may be used, provided that this is done in the light of the same Christian
principles. The Conference records its strong condemnation of the use of
any methods of contraception-control from motives of selfishness, luxury
or mere convenience." (The Lambeth Conferences, 1867-1930, London,
S.P.C.K., 1948) In 1959 the World Council of Churches, in a report on
"Responsible Parenthood and the Population Problem," was more specific
with regard to methods. The Council's statement reads in part: ". . . there
appears to be no moral distinction between the means now known and
practised by the use whether of estimated periods of infertility, or of
artificial barriers to the meeting of sperm and ovum, or indeed, of drugs
which would, if made effective and safe, inhibit or control ovulation in
a calculable way. It remains that the means employed be acceptable to
both husband and wife in Christian conscience, and that, on the best
evidence available, they do neither physical or emotional harm." (*The
Ecumenical Review,* Geneva, Oct. 1959, pp. 85-92.)

measures by the male spouse, under any circumstances." Should the health of the wife be jeopardised, certain birth control measures "are allowed, but only through direct consultation between the medical and rabbinic authorities." [3]

The Roman Catholic Church's teaching that the practice of contraception is a grave sin was spelled out by Pope Pius XI in *Casti Connubii,* where he said:

> But no reason, however grave may be put forward by which anything instrinsically against nature may become comformable to nature and morally good. Since, therefore, the conjugal act is destined primarily by nature for the begetting of children, those who in exercising it deliberately frustrate its natural power and purpose sin against nature and commit a deed which is shameful and intrinsically vicious.

"Small wonder, therefore," Pius XI continued, "if Holy Writ bears witness that the Divine Majesty regards with greatest detestation this horrible crime and at times has punished it with death. As St. Augustine notes, 'Intercourse even with one's legitimate wife is unlawful and wicked where the conception of the offspring is prevented. Onan, the son of Judah, did this and the Lord killed him for it.'" [4]

The doctrine reaffirmed thirty-four years ago by Pius XI that Onan's sin in spilling his seed affords Scriptural authority for the Church's view of contraception as a mortal sin, was underscored by Cardinal Suenens in his book *Love and Control.* There he declares: "She [the Church] will never say that the use of contraceptives is licit. Onanism was condemned in no uncertain terms in *Casti Connubii* which recalled all the Church's traditional teaching on the subject. What was condemned as intrinsically immoral yesterday will not become moral tomorrow . . ." [5]

At least some of the Church's moral theologians today question whether the story of Onan, Genesis XXXVIII, 8-10, can be considered indisputable Scriptural authority for the

Church's teaching on contraception.* Conceding that most moralists still follow this scriptural argument, the Jesuit Fathers Ford and Kelly in their recent book, *Marriage Questions,* state that the matter is "still not perfectly clear."

"Among both Catholic and non-Catholic exegetes," they write, "good arguments can be found for the assertion that Onan was slain for his sin against chastity; and this would mean that at least the immorality of *coitus interruptus* is explicity revealed; and from this we might draw the conclusion that the immorality of other forms of contraception is implicity revealed. But there are other competent exegetes who prefer the interpretation that Onan was slain for his refusal to raise up posterity to his brother. It seems, therefore, that the interpretation that God killed Onan solely or primarily for his sexual sin is not so clearly established that one can assert that there is certainly a divine revelation on this point." [6] †

* It will be noted, in the discussion which follows, that Father Duhamel in his essay, *The Catholic Church and Birth Control,* does not base his interpretation of the natural law on Genesis, 38, 8-10. He nevertheless writes: "My personal opinion is that the detestable thing for which he [Onan] was slain by God was mainly, if not exclusively, the sin of contraception. There are, however, scriptural exegetes who hold that the punishment was inflicted on Onan because of his violation of the Levirate law. But, since death was not a punishment established for the violation of the Levirate law, the fact that Onan was so punished should indicate that it was rather because of his contraceptive act that 'the Lord slew him.'" (p. 21)

† Louis Dupré Associate Professor of Philosophy and Theology at Georgetown University, writes in his book *Contraception and Catholics:* "It is noteworthy that ancient theologians, in dealing with the moral problems of onanism and fornication solved them, not in terms of the isolated act, but in terms of the good of mankind, the population of the world, which, until very recently, was an unqualified good. In the *Summa Contra Gentiles.* St. Thomas [Aquinas] draws the discussion on fornication away from the loss of semen and the conservation of the individual, and places it in the perspective of the propagation of the species. This argument applied to birth control seems to be much more solid. Yet its validity depends on the fact that propagation of the species is an unqualified good, which it certainly was in an agrarian society chronically suffering from underpopulation. Is it still valid today? And, what is of greater urgency, will it still be valid tomorrow everywhere? . . ." (pp. 82-93)

Referring to "the crucial question of how to apply the text of Genesis XXXVIII, 9-10, to the problems and difficulties of married people of our time," the Rev. Bernard Häring, C.Ss.R., author of *The Law of Christ,* said this about Onanism in his colloquy at the University of Notre Dame:

> Can those generous couples who wish to have the maximum number of children they can honestly and properly bring up be charged like Onan who betrayed Thamar, the widow of his brother and his whole kinship by denying her any right of child and by desiring the property of his brother as his own?
>
> There is no doubt that the basic principle of *Casti Connubii,* "What is essentially against nature can never and for no reason be justified as morally good," remains intact. However, the use of the biblical argument (Genesis 38:9f) in *Casti Connubii* does not prove what it wished to prove. The situation and the intention of married couples who have good and sometimes absolutely obligating reasons not to desire a pregnancy are totally different from the situation of Onan, who was killed by God because of the betrayal of his wife and of his kinship.[7]

Father Häring's view that Onanism, or withdrawal, is not under every circumstance a mortal sin is shared by the Belgian theologian, the Rev. Paul Anciaux, former President of the Grand Seminary of Malines. Father Anciaux notes that the Directory for the Administration of the Sacraments, as approved by the Bishops of France in 1951, advises priests "to distinguish onanists who wish to avoid another pregnancy through pure selfishness, from those who have imperative reasons for not desiring another child." At the same time, the Directory stresses that "in no case is Onanism, considered *objectively,* only a venial sin." From this text it must follow, Father Anciaux reasons, that "there are cases where the practice of withdrawal is not a mortal sin on the subjective level." [8]

Fathers Ford and Kelly raise the question whether "the immorality of contraception" is not *"implicitly* revealed in certain [other] Scriptural passages." "Might not," they suggest, "St. Paul's repudiation of one or several unnatural sex practices [I Cor. VI, 9-10] be taken to include implicitly a condemnation of other unnatural sex practices that are not mentioned explicitly? If such an interpretation is correct, then the immorality of at least some forms of contraception (*coitus interruptus* and condomistic intercourse) would be implicitly revealed.

"A third possibility," the Jesuit scholars continue, "is that the entire natural law is *implicitly* contained in the revelation of the two great commandments [St. Matt. XXII, 37-40] and of the Decalogue. When we consider that explanations of the various commandments have consistently included within the scope of each . . . many distinct acts of virtue and many vices not explicitly mentioned . . . this possibility seems to merit further consideration by theologians. One apparent objection that might be raised . . . is the fact that popes, in explaining the Church's right to teach the moral law, have often clearly distinguished between the natural law and revealed moral precepts . . ."—this, despite "the fact that some of the natural law (e.g. the Decalogue) is explicitly revealed. . . ."

It seems to Fathers Ford and Kelly that "the real purpose of such [papal] assertions is to vindicate the Church's power to teach and to apply the natural law, whether it be revealed or not. . . ." [9]

Apart from—or perhaps partly because of—the doubts raised as to Scriptural authority for condemnation of contraception, the Church's philosophical concept of the natural law is difficult for numbers of Catholics, as well as non-Catholics to comprehend.

In an essay written for the laity, "The Catholic Church and Birth Control," now available in pamphlet form, the Rev. Joseph S. Duhamel, S.J., Professor of Moral Theology at Woodstock College, observes:

> . . . it is within the ambience of changing moral views on such problems that the Catholic must lead his social, business, professional, cultural, and religious life in this country. At each of these levels he finds himself in conflict with a large proportion of his fellow countrymen because of certain intransigent positions of that Church which he believes to be the Church of Christ and whose authority to teach in matters of morals as well as of faith he acknowledges. Yet he may wonder, at times, why his Church cannot adapt its teaching to changed modern circumstances. In such difficult interpersonal relationships, it may help the interior peace of the Catholic if he has some understanding of the unchanging and unchangeable principles of reason and revelation on which the Church bases its teaching.

First, Father Duhamel explains that the Church uses the condemnatory term "artificial birth control" not because artificial practices are inherently immoral—hearing aids, for instance, are not—but because the phrase clearly distinguishes "the illegitimate means of limiting the family size from the justified practice of periodic continence."

Next, the Woodstock moral theologian points out, "in the Papal documents contraceptive practices are condemned because 'they are contrary to the law of God and nature.'" "The reference to the law of nature," Father Duhamel continues, "is to a law of God that differs from other divine laws only by reason of the manner in which it is promulgated. One source of our knowledge of God's will is His revelation, as found in Scripture and tradition. But revelation is not the only source of truth. A study of human nature itself, if taken in its completeness with all its internal and external relationships and in conjunction with revelation, is another way in which we can learn God's will about how human beings should direct and govern their actions. This study reveals the natural law, which is God's own law promulgated to man by the light of reason.

"The nature of man," Father Duhamel continues, "is simply his essence, the way he is essentially constituted, looked upon as his ultimate purpose of operation.

> The natural law is the statement of the inner principles of action, placed in man by God in making man what he is, and demanded by the very nature of man so that his human activity may direct him to that perfection which is proper to his human nature.[10]

In other words, man must strive toward perfection in order to be true to the human nature which God has given him. In the marital state he seeks perfection by recognizing, in Father Duhamel's words, that *"that act only is the legitimate expression of conjugal love which is objectively in accord with God's plan for the use of the generative faculty. . . ."*

"Marriage, then, has for its purpose," Father Duhamel explains, "not only the procreation and education of children, but also the individual and united good of the husband and wife. . . .

"Now the realization of the personalist values in marriage has been called by the Church the secondary purpose of the sacrament." Continuing, he writes:

> We must understand, however, that as here used, secondary does not mean unimportant or accidental . . . becoming more united in married love is of tremendous value for its own sake and for the part it plays in the rearing of children. . . .
> The secondary purpose is so much a part of the essence of marriage that the primary purpose can be realized in the

perfect manner intended by God only through the pursuit of the secondary purposes also.[11] *

Cardinal Suenens writes in *Love and Control,* "We have to remember that when the Church calls procreation and its necessary corollary, education, the primary end, she means that this is the most specific of the ends of the conjugal community which unites two people of different sexes. All the other ends pay regard to this orientation which is . . . inherent in all genital activity. . . .

> Therefore, this does not at all mean that the other ends as well are not of first-rank importance. Nor does it mean that the primary end is necessarily the uppermost on the psychological plane . . . the immediate end, felt as first, will be the mutual perfection and complementation of the couple. The most social end—the propagation of the race—will then become a more remote goal . . .[12]

* The Rev. Paul M. Quay, S.J., of West Baden College—to whom Father Duhamel expresses his indebtedness as well as to Fathers Ford and de Lestapis—finds procreation "the most essential but least excellent end." In *Theological Studies,* Vol. 22, 1961, Father Quay writes: "Although the terms 'primary end' and 'secondary end' of marriage are in standard use today, their sense is perhaps best revealed by . . . St. Thomas" who "distinguishes sharply between the more, or less, *essential* ends of marriage (i.e., pertaining to what is constitutive of marriage) and its more, or less, excellent ends. The drive from the twofold sexuality of human nature, through *copula,* to the child leads to the most essential end, the new human. Were there no such sexual process, there would be no question of the special type of human love institutionalized in marriage. Nevertheless, this physiological end is the least excellent of all the ends of marriage and therefore least ultimate. The far loftier ends of sex and marriage presuppose the lower ordination but elevate it and transmute it by reason of their superiority. It is of some interest to note that in the Church's *Rituale,* in all the beautiful marriage ceremony, there is only one brief reference, in the final prayer after the marriage itself is over, to the procreation of children. The nuptial Mass contains several references to children, but they receive little emphasis; here also it is the mutual love and total companionship which gain all the stress. In fine, then, the most essential but least excellent end of marriage is called 'the primary end' because it is the natural goal of the process constituting conjugal relations; it is that which first must be, but only so that it may be transmuted." (pp. 33-34)

Fathers Ford and Kelly put it this way: "The essential subordination of the secondary ends does not mean that they are less essential than the primary ends, if the word essential is understood as we understand it. We call essential that without which marriage cannot exist. . . . There can be degrees of importance. But there can be no degrees of essentialness. . . ."

Noting that St. Augustine's theory of marriage was that procreation was its only end [or justification] the two Jesuit scholars comment, "But the theologians nowadays, and for a long time past, in their theoretical exposition of the ends of marriage, and in their practical teachings on the morality of conjugal intimacy, have broken with the idea that the secondary ends are subordinate to the primary in the sense that they can be justified only when they are a means to the attainment of the primary ends. . . ." [13]

In the words of Father Häring, procreation "is the most specifying end of marriage and of married love . . . a *yes* to the unity and indissolubility of a love which is ordained to the service of life."

But the German theologian points out:

> . . . our natural law arguments against contraception are not understood or accepted by the majority because of . . . lack of necessary study [by theologians] of the sociological, economic, cultural situation, and the psychological and moral attitude of the people of today . . . married people of today consider the problems of marriage fundamentally in terms of conjugal love, and they consider the natural law arguments, neglecting the reality of married love and relegating it to a secondary and nonessential place, as unrealistic and even immoral.[14]

It should be noted that the theologians quoted above, Fathers Ford, Kelly, and Duhamel, find conjugal love *essential,* and that Cardinal Suenens declares it to be "of first-rank importance."

Father Häring calls for positive emphasis on "married love" as being "the most basic condition for the right service of love and for the right procreation and education of the children." He declares: "Both the encounter with modern psychological attitudes and the development of the doctrine of spirituality of marriage demand a doctrinal and pastoral approach which emphasizes the high importance of conjugal love and the necessity of cultivating married love."

These considerations, Father Häring continues, "should not be considered as making for an easier moral code." Instead they "constitute a nobler and stronger challenge to married people to watch over the purity and vitality of their love in the conjugal act as well as in the whole of the married and domestic life. . . .

> A natural law consideration which places the accent only on a right biological performance of the conjugal act remains on the level of mere animals and considers as primary what man has in common with the animals. It forgets the higher needs of the persons and therefore remains a very poor minimalism.[15]

With "the higher needs of the persons" very much in mind, Father Duhamel reasons that "in the very exercise of the marital act there is a symbolism that is important for the understanding of the Church's position. . . ." He explains:

> The act of intercourse is the external symbol of internal union. Of its very nature it says: I love you; I give myself to you unreservedly, completely; I give you of myself, of my substance, of that which I am as a man and as a husband, holding nothing back. And, on the part of the wife: I rejoice in this union of our bodies as we are already united in mind and heart; I yield my womanhood and my wifehood to you completely, unreservedly; I am openly receptive to your

substance, to the power of your manhood over me, rejecting no part of you.*

In marital intercourse Father Duhamel sees a second symbolism. The act is:

a natural sign of the willingness to become a father and mother, of the desire to confer on each other the dignity of fatherhood or motherhood, of the common will to be also united in parenthood.

As its third natural symbolism, the marital act expresses:

an openness of both body and will to the creative act of God by which a human being comes into existence. It proclaims, of its very nature, a willingness to cooperate with God in this most sacred of human functions: to provide the physical two-in-one substance into which God, by an immediate creative act, will infuse a human soul.

From "revelation," the author continues, "there emerges a still higher symbolism of the marital act. We are told in the fifth chapter of the Epistle to the Ephesians that the sacrament of marriage is the symbol of the union of Christ and His Church, . . . a total gift on the part of Christ of the abundance of His graces which man must not render fruitless by his refusal to cooperate with them." [16]

This being the Church's immemorial concept of marriage, Father Duhamel explains at different points in his essay why the Church condemns birth control: †

* Agreeing that the physical act of intercourse is a symbol of surrender, Louis Dupré comments: "Yet this spiritual significance does not necessarily imply that the material act is simply to be accepted from nature, and that if it is at all modified it must lose its meaning altogether . . . Man receives his symbols from nature, but at the same time he *lives* them and, in living them, transforms them. A symbol which is not concretely lived is no longer a symbol; it becomes an empty shell. . . ." (*Contraception and Catholics,* p. 70)

† Alphabetical ordering supplied.

a. "Human beings may not choose to start a process which reason and revelation tell them has procreation as an essential purpose while they destroy this central purpose, by human artifice . . .

b. While a couple may have sufficient reason "to justify a responsible decision to have no more children . . . the morality of the means . . . must also be considered. . . . It is not left to the arbitrary decision of human beings to choose any means of their own preference as the expression of their love. . . ."

c. "Man does not have absolute ownership of his own life, nor of his body, nor of the organs and functions of his body. In their regard he is only a steward and he is bound . . . to use them only for the purposes ordained by God . . ."

d. ". . . it is immoral to contravene any essential purpose of marriage, whether it be primary or secondary. . . ." While the Church does subordinate the secondary to the primary, "this . . . is not a necessary element for the justification of the Church's position . . . when contraceptives are used . . . something is held back—and in that holding back, the complete two-in-oneship of the husband and wife is prevented as surely as conception is prevented. This is a violation of the secondary purpose of marriage . . ."

e. ". . . the marital act is not intended to be a closed union of dual egocentricity, each seeking to satisfy the other to the exclusion of every other consideration. . . . There is the use of the sign that says parenthood while deliberately destroying its meaning in its very use. . . . It is a distortion of the second natural symbolism of the marital act."

f. ". . . contraception rejects . . . openness to God's creative intervention in the very act that speaks it . . . the third natural symbolism of the marital act is destroyed . . ."

g. ". . . if it is lawful to separate completely the procreative purpose of the generative function and of the marital act from their personalist and individual values," then there is "no principle by which any mutual act of two people, married or unmarried, of opposite sexes or of the same sex, can be condemned as immoral . . ."[17]

Father de Lestapis, in his book, *Family Planning and Modern Problems,* lists five reasons why birth regulation by the rhythm method, as contrasted with artificial birth control, is consonant with the natural law. In summary they are:

1. Regulation is a code of conduct; birth control, a technic. "It is a code based on the actual structure of female sexuality," one that calls on male sexuality "to confine its inseminatory activity to the days when the female organs are at rest, and this out of respect and love for its partner. Contraceptive birth control . . . disregards nature's directions and overrides them. . . ."

2. Regulation gives priority to *quality;* birth control to *quantity.* . . . "Contraceptive control . . . seems to stake everything . . . on the number of sexual relations. . . . It therefore does not seem capable of giving to the couple, in addition to sensual pleasure, either the enriching joy of the effort towards self-mastery or the spiritual reward of a personal and mutually agreed control over instinct."

3. ". . . birth regulation is opposed to contraceptive control as *art* is to *artifice.* Contraception . . . presents itself simply as a 'prescription,' an 'appliance,' . . . so the supposed mutual self-giving relation . . . runs the grave risk of sinking to the level of a reciprocal technique or more often a technique directed exclusively to giving the husband satisfaction . . . birth regulation . . . presupposes a whole pattern of life . . . demands a genuine education. This is why it is in the sphere of art and not that of artifice. It makes us free of the profound joys of art, joys . . . not merely pleasures. . . . Pleasure is only an artifice Nature has devised to ensure that living creatures hand

on the gift of life. It does not point out the direction in which life is to move. . . ."

4. "Birth regulation leads the way to the kingdom of the 'open universe.' Birth control immures us in the 'closed universe.' " It was Bergson who taught that "those who take up their abode in 'a closed well-being'—which they imagine will be permanent—run a very great risk of finally succumbing to boredom and of sinking into an empty, isolated existence. Those . . . who open their hearts to self-transcending vocation, find joy in progress and discovery. . . ."

5. "Birth regulation is, of its nature, *compatible with the spiritual life:* birth control, in practice, takes no account of this life." [18]

In Father Duhamel's words, practice of periodic continence is "an act of love of God, because it is precisely out of reverence for the law of God . . . that the husband and wife abstain when sexual intercourse with contraceptives would be so much easier a solution.

"The morality of the means used in the exercise of responsible parenthood," the scholar concludes, "is of prime importance. The Church sees in the method of periodic continence a legitimate means; but she has always, and with good reason, condemned contraceptive practices as intrinsically evil and a violation of the law of God." [19] *

* Concerning the morality of the means used, the Jesuit magazine, *America,* in an editorial on "Fertility and Control," in its Jan. 4, 1964 issue, said in part: "That a couple may legitimately use periodic continence is not a new idea in Catholic thought. What is new is a willingness to accept periodic continence as more than an exceptional and emergency practice. . . . This development in Catholic moral attitudes has been hailed in certain quarters as a step toward full approval of contraception as a moral practice. Many persons, including some highly intelligent ones, say that they see no difference between contraception and periodic continence, both being means to the same end. That may mean no more than that they subscribe to the utilitarianism that is the working moral philosophy of our age. The essence of utilitarianism is that it prescinds from the intrinsic moral evaluation of acts and judges them by what, strictly speaking, is outside them: their utility, their results.

Compassionately recognizing that to obey the Church's teaching is often very difficult, Father de Lestapis comments:

> And yet, if we throw ourselves into Christ's arms, chastity will gradually become possible. It will issue from the dialogue we have begun with Him, a dialogue which involves on our part a spirit of generosity, but also lapses, sufferings, doubts, moments of weariness. . . . And so we eventually cease to worry very much about these lapses, when we have chosen Christ. We do not think God is very angry with us if we sometimes happen to go beyond the lawful bounds through some sudden impulse or because of our weakness. The only thing to do is to ask at once for forgiveness, for if we return to Him and to our dialogue with Him, He is always ready to receive us, is kind, welcoming, our friend.[20]

"There can be merely imperfection, conscious venial sin or mortal sin," Father Häring, declares: ". . . one puts himself in the most extreme danger if he does not strive towards the deep respect for the mystery of marriage and sexuality and towards the self-control which safeguards the expression of this respect. But the lack of striving can have very different degrees. . . ."

> We should not consider as mortal sinners couples who are generous in their judgment as to responsible parenthood, who are living in real charity and generosity and praying for perserverance; we should not consider them as mortal sinners, if, in spite of good will, they do not yet understand all the needs of a full conjugal chastity and if they do not even obtain the perfect performance of what they understand as a need of the virtue of conjugal chastity.

That, perhaps, is why so many intellectuals are blind to the difference between periodic continence and contraception. But the Church sees a fundamental difference, and there is no reason to assume that she will one day cease to see it. What we can expect is increasing Catholic support for study of the human reproductive system. . . ."

"Here we could remember," Father Häring continues, "The wonderful words of St. Augustine. . . . 'A man cannot so quickly reach the heights of justice as when he has fallen down from it. Even though he is already in the Church (in the inn of redemption), he still needs help. . . .'" [21] *

* For a dissenting view on the natural law, presented by Professor Dupré of Georgetown University, see pp. 133-138.

Four | Practice of the Rhythm Method

Rythm

"Birth regulation," writes the French family sociologist, Father de Lestapis, in *Family Planning and Modern Problems,* "presupposes in any case complete or temporary continence, periodic or lasting for a considerable time, practised by mutual agreement between husband and wife and organized in accordance with nature and the actual characteristics of the female organism. . . ." [1]

It was more than thirteen years ago that Pius XII explicitly approved of the natural method of birth regulation when a couple's motives are moral. Yet there are still Catholics in this country who condemn the use of rhythm. In this connection, Father Thomas of St. Louis University writes in *Marriage and Rhythm*:

> It is difficult to understand the mentality of those who spend more time and energy in attacks on rhythm than on con-

traceptives. Either they are wholly unaware of present social conditions and the successes of the "planned parenthooders," or they fail to appreciate the complexities of sex in marriage when they so lightly recommend total abstinence . . .[2]

This situation is gradually, if slowly, changing. In a series of articles published in the summer of 1963 by the *New York Times,* based on interviews with Catholic theologians, educators, scientists and editors, George Barrett writes that "priests are being called in by some dioceses for briefings on the new affirmative emphasis by the Church on family planning and limitation." For most priests, he reports, this is a "revolutionary turn."

In Buffalo, in 1961, the Most Rev. Joseph A. Burke, late Bishop of the Diocese, approved the setting up of a Catholic rhythm clinic, the first in the nation. Today a rotating staff of 25 specialists instruct women in rhythm control five nights a week. Priests and physicians come from other dioceses to take a close look.[3]

In 1962, a rhythm clinic was established at St. Vincent's Hospital in New York City, not only to instruct women but to find whether the method can be simplified and perfected.* Recently rhythm clinics have been opened by four other Catholic hospitals, covering the five boroughs.

The biologic basis of the rhythm method—and its present limitations—are explained in detail by Father Thomas in his book. He points out that the exact determination in advance of a woman's day of ovulation each month "is clearly essential if conception is to be avoided. . . ."

Two methods of pinpointing ovulation have gained prominence,—the Ogino-Knaus method, and the body temperature method. The former, Father Thomas explains, is based on two important assumptions:

* See pp. 172-173.

(1) that ovulation regularly takes place on the 15th day before the onset of menstruation

(2) in the average woman, the *pattern* of the menstrual cycle is uniform and can be predicted.

How well-founded, Father Thomas asks, is this assumption of a predictable monthly cycle pattern? "It appears," he writes, "that under normal circumstances a good proportion of women develop a definite monthly cycle pattern." But the range is wide—from the "few who have absolutely regular periods," to those who may have a variation every month of only two or three days, to others who may vary by as much as ten days—and finally to "some women who never develop a definite pattern. . . ." For this reason, Father Thomas notes:

> In practice, doctors who supervise this method put little trust in women's memory. . . . They uniformly insist that their clients mark down the date of onset and keep accurate records for a period of roughly one year, so that their individual patterns may be determined.

Unusual conditions, the author cautions, "may disturb the pattern either temporarily or for a longer period of time." Such conditions as:

mental or physical over-exertion
excessive emotional experience
sudden changes of climate, altitude or occupation
marked glandular disturbances
some physical and mental illnesses
the menopause

"Finally," Father Thomas adds, "the period following a pregnancy . . . generally reveals some menstrual irregularity. Particularly during the lactation period, menstruation frequently stops for some time. . . ." For this reason, he explains, doctors generally insist on observing the menstrual pattern for two or three months to see whether it has changed.

It follows, the author continues, that except after a pregnancy and in the absence of other possible disturbances, "conception can be promoted or prohibited by engaging in or abstaining from marital relations during the two or three days preceding and during the estimated ovulation period in the cycle." He suggests this numerical formula for calculating the fertile period:

> For a woman with a 24-30 day cycle, the period of fertility would extend for ten days—from the seventh to the 17th of her cycle.

The second commonly used method of fixing the time of ovulation is the body temperature method. This calls for a woman's charting her temperature every morning before she arises or engages in any other activity, for a period of three to six months. While there is some difference of opinion among researchers, Father Thomas writes, "most agree . . . there is a perceptible rise . . . during or immediately after ovulation and that each woman will display her own pattern of increase. . . ."

"Proponents of this method," Father Thomas notes, "believe that all but about 10 percent of married women can rely on the basal temperature chart in determining their period of ovulation." [4]

Without himself appraising the temperature method, Cardinal Suenens reports in his book, *Love and Control,* the highly favorable findings of three European specialists, Drs. J. Holt, G. K. Döring and M. Chartier, findings based, respectively, on 200, 5,000, and 1,025 cases. The Belgian cardinal comments:

> If unanimous agreement is reached on these conclusions, it will be more than ever necessary for doctors, working through trained assistants, to teach the proper use of the method and to make it widely known. No matter what it is, every method presupposes a certain, minimal knowledge,

and doctors tell us that ignorance on this subject is unbelievable.[5]

Father de Lestapis recommends that young couples before they marry seek information about the body temperature method "either from a marriage guidance center or from an *experienced* doctor." He reasons:

> It is an undoubted fact that the more accurately and exactly the future wife is able to diagnose her period every month and even perhaps the actual day when ovulation begins, the more natural and easy will be the regulation of births when it becomes necessary. . . .[6]

To disseminate authentic information about the body temperature method, Father de Lestapis, wth a group of French doctors, founded in July, 1961 the *Centre de Liason des Equipes de Recherche.* Through its nationwide program the Center seeks to educate not only married couples in the scientific, psychological and spiritual aspects of the temperature method, but also doctors and nurses, priests, nuns and social workers.

In an article published in the May 2, 1964 issue of *America,* the Rev. Arthur W. Kane, a New Englander now studying in Europe, reports on the French Center's far-flung activities. The C.L.E.R. staff in Paris correlates and publishes research data on the body temperature method. In 12 major French cities fully-staffed C.L.E.R. centers instruct couples seeking advice. At a still lower level, some fifty "teams" travel over France, teams composed typically of a doctor, a priest and a married couple experienced in the temperature method of birth regulation. Couples—non-Catholic as well as Catholic— are instructed in group sessions. At the first session, various contraceptive measures are objectively treated; at the second, the temperature method is explained in detail, and at a third session, psychological-spiritual motivation is discussed. Supplementing the teams, "instructor couples" acquaint their neighbors, from their experience and through informal guidance, with the use of the temperature method.

As taught in the C.L.E.R. program, Father Kane explains:

> Continence must be practised for at least 11 days: seven days for the normal period of fertility and four days for the average menstruation period. Depending on the degree of security required, continence can be prolonged to 16 days in an average cycle of 28 days when the couple avoid using the first period of the cycle following menstruation. The period of conjugal relations will vary, therefore, from 12 to 17 days according to whether the period of relative sterility is used or not.

One of the first French physicians to postulate the importance of basal temperature changes was Dr. R. Palmer of the University of Paris, a Protestant, whose research began in 1938 with a study of the causes of sterility. "Recently," Father Kane reports, "in a paper read before the Societe Nationale pour L'Etude de la Sterilite et de la Fecondite, Dr. Palmer asserted that the restriction of conjugal relations to the hyperthermal plateau [when the temperature curve remains high] meant 99 percent security against fecundation. Other European researchers, such as Drs. Holt, Chartier, Ferin and Vincent, have affirmed similar results. . . ."

The C.L.E.R. program, Father Kane adds, has been extended beyond France. In 1963 Father de Lestapis and a corps of physicians carried it to five major cities in India and to Réunion and Mauritius, islands in the Indian ocean. In Singapore the Catholic Medical Guild promotes the education and motivation of people of all faiths in the temperature method. In Montreal a group of laymen and doctors have since the 1950's been counseling couples on the use of the temperature method and have formed an organization similar to C.L.E.R., known as SERENA. In Great Britain, the Catholic Marriage Advisory Council offers instruction in the temperature method at its 60 centers.[7]

In his comments on the body temperature method, Father Thomas points out that [since a woman's temperature does not rise until ovulation has occurred] "it does not appear to be a reliable method for avoiding conception" at that period of the cycle. Since the male sperm is believed by most scientists to remain vital for at least 48 hours after ejaculation, conception could occur if marital relations had taken place the day before ovulation.* Use of the body temperature method in conjunction with the Ogino-Knaus method, Father Thomas suggests, "could prove very helpful in cases where the cycle pattern reveals a wide variation."

Summing up what is known about the rhythm method, Father Thomas states: "There seems sufficient evidence to indicate that when rhythm is practised by intelligent women in accordance with . . . prescriptions . . . it is highly effective. . . ."

In the present state of knowledge, Father Thomas asserts, "there is no method, short of total abstinence . . . which can absolutely guarantee that a couple capable of procreation will not conceive a child." It follows that

> if the life of the mother would be seriously threatened by another pregnancy, continency rather than rhythm should be advised.

When the rhythm method is practicable, there are three prerequisites to its licit use, Father Thomas stresses. The husband and wife must agree on the necessary limitation of the marital rights of each. They must have a moral reason.

* The accepted medical opinion has been that sperm cells present in the vaginal tract retain their potency for no longer than 48 hours. That in some cases they may remain capable of impregnation for a longer period was disclosed in a 3-year research study conducted at the Albert Einstein Medical Center in Philadelphia and reported in the *American Journal of Obstetrics and Gynecology*. Forty-four women were included in the study. Among nine, significant numbers of active spermatazoa were found in mucus of the cervix—the neck of the uterus—five days after insemination; in one woman, after six days, and in still another, after seven days. (*N.Y. Times*, Feb. 16, 1964.)

And they must "be capable of bearing the tension and restraint which the practice of rhythm may involve." He explains:

> If the restriction of marital relations . . . places either partner in the proximate occasion of sinning against chastity, or if the accompanying tension seriously threatens the growth of mutual love and harmony . . . the use of rhythm is illicit.

"Sexual response in the normal man and woman," Father Thomas writes, "is not directly under the control of the will. This means that if the stimulus is received, the normal adult responds automatically." For this reason, he notes, prudent counselors advice "the avoidance of the stimulus (fleeing the occasion)." "To avoid the occasion" in the normal marriage state "is not easy," Father Thomas grants. Frustration may shorten tempers, and "criticism of the partner tends to take on an unaccustomed sharpness."

Father Thomas grants, too, that there "is generally considerable uncertainty and worry about pregnancy." If the rhythm method fails, "in our contemporary pagan atmosphere there is real danger that the couple will look on pregnancy as an unfortunate frustration of their plans and upon children as an unnecessary burden in marriage."

What married couples need, Father Thomas reasons, is "a thoughtful restatement of the meaning of life in the terms of Catholic values and contemporary living conditions." "They need to understand that their legitimate aspirations for self-development and self-realization coincide with the obligations of parenthood." Also, "their faith must be enlivened" so that they will trust to "the sacramental graces" to give them strength.[8]

"There is, however, one big difficulty about the practice of periodic continence," the already quoted theologian, Father Häring, observes in an article published in the May 29, 1964, issue of *The Catholic Reporter*, "Distinguishing between fertile and infertile days is possible only when the monthly cycle is regular and when a woman has both the intelligence and the leisure to keep track of its regular variations between fertility and infertility.

> When the cycle is totally irregular, a married couple are in dire straits as regards exercising responsible parenthood. The same problem arises when the husband has to work in separation from his family, as in the case of so many Italians who work in northern Europe and return home for a few days now and then, often only once a year. They have very serious reasons for not wishing a new pregnancy to result from their short visit home to wives, yet their visit may correspond with the fertile days of a struggling and lonely wife. What is to be done in such cases?

There are couples, Father Häring continues, who "have trained themselves with time—it may have taken a long time —to live in marriage without . . . intercourse, showing their affection and love for each other in a thousand little tendernesses. . . . This kind of married love, is however, easier as a rule for a wife to accept and bear than for a husband. A wife feels more for the husband she loves than for herself in such a case. His long day is spent outside the home toiling for her and for the home; she has at least the advantage of living her life in the personal atmosphere of the home." [9]

From the standpoint of a philosopher, Dr. Dupré of Georgetown University, writes in *Contraception and Catholics:*

> It would seem to me that the meaning of the act of marriage is determined not only by the totality of man's spiritual life, but also by the fact that he has to express his love in a repetition of acts over a period of time. . . . To deprive the act permanently or constantly of its tendency toward procreation, would definitely imply a basic reservation in the surrender and thus contradict the objective meaning of the marital act. . . . But for two marriage partners who have

repeatedly proven their intention of complete surrender in creative acts of love, to exclude occasionally the fertility of their love when circumstances prevent them from taking proper care of new offspring, does not necessarily contradict the objective meaning of the marital act. . . .[10]

A sociologist at the University of Notre Dame, Dr. William V. D'Antonio, an associate professor, asks "What is the problem with rhythm?" in a full-page article on conjugal love and responsible parenthood published April 3, 1964 by *The Catholic Reporter,* the Kansas City diocesan weekly.

Answering, he writes:

The primary problem is that of the duration of the period of continence required. For a small percentage of couples a period of only five or six days of abstinence is required. This short period . . . is generally not burdensome. In fact, it may be beneficial . . . abstinence makes the heart grow fonder. But for the great majority, periods of from 10 to 15 days or more of abstinence may be required, and this is where conjugal love is jeopardized. Many couples are wondering how continence in these circumstances can be a higher good than conjugal union.

"A University of Michigan fertility control study," Dr. D'Antonio notes, "using a U.S. national sample showed that about half of the Catholic couples in the study who used any control used only rhythm. . . . But the scientists also learned that there was a clear-cut pattern by which Catholics, once they had achieved the family size desired or found themselves with a larger family than desired, resorted to contraceptives . . . the more education the Catholic couple had, the more rhythm was likely to be resorted to exclusively. However, even one-third of the college-educated who admitted to trying to regulate fertility, resorted to the use of contraceptives." [11] *

* A survey of 2700 women under 40 years of age was conducted by Ronald Freedman, Professor of Sociology and Research Associate of the Survey Research Center, University of Michigan; Pascal K. Whelpton,

In the practice of rhythm, Cardinal Suenens observes, a married couple must have "faith that self-control can be achieved." "Believing that one can succeed is essential to success. . . ." He points out that "more and more psychologists underline the influence of the soul on the body, of the psychic on the physical." Modern psychophysiologists, practitioners of a relatively new science, the Cardinal notes, postulate that a human being's sex, unlike an animal's, "lies more in his brain than in his hormones."

But the Belgian Cardinal advances the opinion that all couples need not necessarily practice a rigid ascetism during the period of continence. He writes:

> An "all or nothing" attitude is not a good solution because it will work for some strong souls, but is not the ordinary and normal way. Married couples must be able to translate their love into physical activity and gestures even though they are obliged to abstain from the final act of love.[12]

In the same connection Father de Lestapis observes:

> Certain couples may even find it to their advantage during the fertile period to make use—after giving it a trial—of the intercourse known as *copula reservata* with the self-control it makes possible. . . . Experience will have taught them that there can be an invigorating joy . . . [when they are] content to keep their emotions on the level of a loving, tender and sensitive affection. They purposely prevent them from reaching the point where nature automatically

Director, Scripps Foundation for Research in Population Problems, Miami University, and Arthur A. Campbell, Assistant Professor, Scripps Foundation. Of the 787 Catholic women included in the survey, fertility control had been attempted in 453 marriages. Among these, 47 per cent of the couples had used only the rhythm method; 24 per cent, only appliance methods; 15 per cent had combined rhythm and appliances; 6 per cent, withdrawal and appliances; 2 per cent, a combination of rhythm and withdrawal, and another 2 per cent had used rhythm, withdrawal and appliances. (*Family Planning Sterility and Population Growth.* New York: McGraw Hill, 1959, p. 184, Table 6-4.)

releases the full sexual mechanism whose action is obviously directed solely to inseminatory intercourse.

Copula reservata is not to be confused with *coitus interruptus,* or withdrawal (onanism), which the Church has always condemned. *Copula reservata* permits male entry but not orgasm. The technique is believed to have been practiced for centuries in the Orient and was adopted by the Oneida Community in the 19th century in this country. Later, European literature discussed the subject.

In 1952—Father de Lestapis explains in a footnote—the Holy Office issued a Monitum forbidding general circulation of Catholic writing on *copula reservata,* but leaving the question open for further scientific study. Noting that the technique now has a somewhat better scientific foundation, he expresses the hope that careful sexological studies will "eventually give a complete answer to this question."

At the same time, Father de Lestapis quotes a fellow French priest as warning against the hope that "we can rescue (married couples) solely by means of a natural solution, when what is needed is . . . an insistence on the need for the self-abnegation demanded of us by revelation." [13]

In this country, the Director of the Family Life Bureau of the Archdiocese of New York, Msgr. George A. Kelly, condemns *coitus (copula) reservatus* in his most recent book, *Birth Control and Catholics.* He writes of the practice:

From the strictly practical point of view *coitus reservatus* has been described as bringing "brinkmanship" to sex. It calls for extremely great control by the male; a control which physicians say is difficult to achieve without strong motivation and considerable practice. . . . From the emotional point of view, this would seem to be a highly undesirable method of expressing love. . . . It is primarily from the moral point of view, of course, that our objections are based . . . it can lead to the "contraceptive mentality," if it is not in fact a direct result of it. . . .[14]

Referring to "the difficult question of birth regulation," Msgr. W. Bekkers, Bishop of 's-Hergentobosch in the Netherlands, in his much-discussed TV speech of March 21, 1963 said that only by a deepening of human experience, does man become able "to apply regulation in such a fashion that it fits in" with the concept of Christian marriage. He said further:

> . . . while we know that periodic continence is a solution for many people, we are also aware that it presents others with really insuperable arguments. We realize too that there may be certain situations in which it is impossible to be mindful of all and every Christian and human value at the same time.
>
> The Church does not consider this from a prejudiced, aloof point of view to be wholly due to selfishness and love of ease—even if, in many cases, this is the inescapable truth. She knows that some, sincerely concerned though they are for their families and each other, sometimes go ways which she cannot recognize as the right ones. But the Church also knows that what is possible for one particular individual is not necessarily within reach of another. She realises that there is room for gradual, though possibly slow and defective, growth as in all the other spheres of life . . .[15]

Bishop Bekkers' view that periodic continence presents many couples "with really insuperable arguments" is not conceded by moral theologians generally, and most certainly not by American moralists. The Rev. Richard A. McCormick, S.J., professor of moral and pastoral theology at West Baden College in Indiana observed in the January 11, 1964 issue of *America*: "As for practical difficulties, many couples experience enormous hardship through the demands of sane conjugal morality. To this suffering, Christianity brings deep sympathy and solace; but it has never apologized for suffering in the world any more than it has removed it. The expression of conjugal love remains at once a mysteriously fragile, a profound, a terrible thing. It will always present a problem to human beings and will never be far from the shadow of the cross. But in facing these problems, is it not as unsound to suppose that the only answer is contraception as it is to suppose that the only answer must be absolute continence? . . . Conjugal love and its associated problems constitute an area where we are peculiarly liable to experience the pains of growth—both by unquestioning adherence to an established formula and by rash abandonment of its essential contents."

Five | The Married Speak

These days an increasing number of married Catholics are overcoming their natural reserve and writing letters to the editors of Catholic publications about their experiences as husbands and wives. Some few have produced thoughtful, highly literate articles. These outpourings in print reflect a wide divergence of viewpoint, a difference in understanding of the Church's teaching on the moral means of achieving responsible parenthood—even a sharp clash over the question whether it is truly Christian to attempt family limitation. All who have sought to share their experiences and deep beliefs write as Catholics who love their Church, whether or not they find understandable, or acceptable, the theologians' interpretation of the natural law.

Mrs. Rosemary Ruether, a teacher of humanities at Scripps College in Claremont, California, initiated a married folks' debate with an article printed in the December, 1963, issue of the Catholic monthly, *Jubilee*. This contribution aroused such interest that Mrs. Ruether's views in different and much stronger form were published in the April 4, 1964, issue of *The Saturday Evening Post* in an article captioned "A Catholic Mother Tells 'Why I Believe in Birth Control'." The mother of three children aged five, four and one, and the wife of a political science professor, Mrs. Ruether writes:

> Not just intellectually but through personal experience I have come to believe that the birth control rulings of the Church are based on inadequate and inaccurate views both of sex in marriage and of family life. . . . For my husband and me, as well as for a great many of the Catholic couples we know, the rhythm method has caused much grief. To most of us it seems theologically meaningless. Worse, we know how it tends to take away the joy and spontaneity from marriage.

A close friend had told Mrs. Ruether that even she, whose husband is a doctor, had had virtually no success with the rhythm method. "I can scarcely forget," Mrs. Ruether writes, "the look of desperation in her eyes when she said,

> I just threw the thermometer away when I found I was pregnant again. This is our sixth child in seven years, and every one has to come by Caesarian section. I just don't know how much more I can take.

"Whenever the period is late," the writer observes, "or the signs by which the woman tries to predict her cycle are off schedule, there is a time of panic. I know of husbands who have exploded in helpless rage and wives who have become hysterical. . . . Many times I have seen parents taking out their fear and resentment on their children. . . .

> Many priests tell parishioners that the only difficulty in the use of rhythm is self-control. . . . What they fail to see is

> . . . that the woman is cast in the role of, literally, the policeman of the marital bed. . . . It is not surprising that after a few years of struggling with such a system, a husband and wife begin to feel their whole marriage somehow twisted. Some women even begin to feel a positive abhorrence of sex . . .

It appears to Mrs. Ruether that "the intent and purpose of an act are the main criteria of its morality." "If," she argues, "it is morally acceptable to divorce sex from impregnation (and this is obviously the intent of the rhythm method), it would then seem to make little difference whether the egg and sperm are separated by barriers of space or of time. . . .

> The weakness of the natural law argument lies in an equivocal use of the word "nature." Nature is used to mean simultaneously both the natural link between sex and impregnation on the biological level and also the ideal nature of the act, and what sex should mean as a part of a loving relationship between two human beings. The Church doctrine simply runs these two meanings together and forbids that they be separated.

"Isn't it possible," this woman teacher concludes, "that the evils of perverting the psychological nature of marriage may be considerably greater than any evils in regulating the biological nature of marriage? Isn't the Church greatly harmed when it forces people to obey a rule they really can't accept and not merely because the rule makes life difficult but, more important, because it doesn't seem to be serving any meaningful moral purpose. . . ."

Support for—and dissent from—Mrs. Ruether's position were registered by Catholic readers in the May 2nd letters-column of *The Saturday Evening Post.* "I couldn't believe," a California mother of three writes, "that someone actually had the nerve to come out and state in a national magazine what most of us are thinking." Another Californian, a young mother of four, deplores "the ridiculous position the Church puts married couples in." An Arizona correspondent says: "After seven years and four babies and nearly ending up mental wrecks... my husband and I finally joined the ranks of many other Catholics who feel that we owe it to the children we already have not to have more until we can cope with more." A New York City man congratulates Mrs. Ruether "for her courage in saying publicly what so many of us have, for far too long, confined to private discussion among our fellow Catholics."

On the other side, a Westchester housewife observes, "If Mrs. Ruether prefers a Ph.D. to another child, why doesn't she say so?" An Ohio woman reader declares, "There are many crosses and disappointments in this life we must bear in order to merit an eternal life. I hope our fifth child in five years will help to be our road to heaven." A Minnesota man observes, "Mrs. Ruether admits that she isn't disciplined enough to be a Catholic. Let her become a Protestant." An Indiana priest comments that Mrs. Ruether appears to have "forgotten her catechism," and that "He didn't create us to enjoy ourselves."

A month after Mrs. Ruether's article appeared in *The Saturday Evening Post, America* magazine printed a full-dress reply —an article captioned "Is It Immature Loving?" written by Frank M. Wessling, a father of five who is the managing editor of *Reign of the Sacred Heart.* Mr. Wessling's theme is that Mrs. Ruether's "real problem"—and that of other "affluent people—is not birth control" but "a static notion of love." [1]

Mr. Wessling grants that "for various reasons, some rooted in Western history and some in the Jansenist plague, Catholic doctrine on marriage has suffered bad explanation . . ." and that "very often the way marriage has been preached has tended to underscore its biological functions at the expense of its total human reality."

"Despite the penitential breast-beating of St. Augustine," Mr. Wessling continues, "total personal union, including sexual union, is the heart of marriage . . . it is this that is at the center of the sacrament—the Christ-finding aspect—of marriage."

Christian marriage, he further observes, "is a promise to make two into one. Two people as different as they can be—man and woman—promise to make an attempt to immerse their separate prior selves into a new self, a synthesis forged in the time-fires of struggle, joy, conflict, pain, ecstasy, fear—all the jolting glory of human life well lived. Two people afraid of life can marry, of course, and have much less of life than this in their love, but then they should not afflict others with their complaints that the half-life isn't satisfactory." As Mr. Wessling sees it, there are myriad intimate ways in which a husband and wife can express their love for each other—"with a touch, a look, a word, as well as with an embrace." If the two, he argues, "have not learned in a few years how to give themselves to each other totally in the intimacy of an understood look, then they had better get busy learning how to love each other. They are simply lousy lovers. And I don't care if they hustle off to bed every night of the week for the so-called marital embrace. If that is the only love-making they do, they are at best only half alive."

Mrs. Ruether is "quite wrong," Mr. Wessling holds, in complaining that the discipline (required by the rhythm method) "is a matter of destroying some positive good in the marital relationship." Since neither Mr. Wessling nor his wife had wanted her to be "a baby machine," they were forced, he recalls, "not to take the easy way—for intercourse is the easy way." "True," he writes,

> it is the seal on married life, but it should not be necessary to be constantly sealing the same empty envelope. My wife and I think there is joy in filling the envelope with all the small daily love-making we can. The seal then takes on fresh meaning each time we impress it upon our lives.

What the Church says about birth control, this contributor to *America,* concedes, "is hard for most people to accept." He thinks it need not be so, however, if it is understood. "The Church says," he points out, "as a witness to the marriage promise of a man and woman . . . that the married couple have no right to renege, or to attach later conditions, on the promise of *total* self-giving. Contraceptive birth control is, purely and simply, the giving of self *with reservation*."

"What the Church can do," he continues, "to make Mrs. Ruether and a host of other people a bit less frustrated is to take most priests out of the business of marriage counselling. Too many who think they have a right to counsel married people simply have no appreciation of married life. . . . I must agree completely with Mrs. Ruether when she expresses exasperation over priests who tell people that 'the only difficulty in the use of rhythm is self-control.' "

Married people must be helped to see "in the proper light," Mr. Wessling writes, "any necessary discipline imposed on marital love." "I have real hope," he concludes, "that the Church will shed a great deal of that light . . . in the future. Bishops like Cardinal Suenens and theologians like Father Bernard Häring are forerunners of the churchmen who will confront the Rosemary Ruethers of the future."

> They will not tell her that "the only difficulty in the use of rhythm is self-control." They will ask her what goes into the total rhythm of her life. They will want to know if she is only playing a one-note tune in her marital love or if she is making an attempt to play a symphony of intimacy. They will not immediately consign her to hell if she is struggling over rugged problems. But they will try to help her see that she doesn't yet know as much as she thinks she knows about growth in marital intimacy.

In her riposte—a letter printed in the May 30, 1964, issue of *America,* Mrs. Ruether finds unpersuasive the reasoning of the Catholic editor. "Mr. Wessling," she writes, "presents the argument . . . that seems to be the new Catholic anti-contraceptive argument. It replaces the old simple-minded 'primary purpose' argument.

"According to this argument," Mrs. Ruether contends, "the marital act is fulfilled only when there is total self-giving, without any reservations. By this the authors seem to mean that there are no reservations of the procreative functions of the act. What the proponents of this argument seem to overlook is that this argument, taken literally, rules out the rhythm method no less than any other method of contraception. It is a kind of totalistic argument that assumes that an act is immoral unless all functions are intentionally present, a criterion which we would hesitate to apply to any other area of our life."

Mrs. Ruether puts these questions:

> . . . what could be more "conditional" self-giving than making love only when you are sterile? What could be more negative than withdrawal from relationship whenever there is a possibility that the act may be fecund? What "reservations" are involved when a couple, in order to even hope for effective use of the rhythm method, must make this the overriding regime of their sexual relationship for some 20 to 25 years?

All methods of birth control, rhythm included, Mrs. Ruether maintains, use the sexual act for "its relational function" and rule out procreation. "Where, then, is the significant difference between methods?" * she challenges Mr. Wessling. "This is the question I asked in my article and which you have not succeeded in answering."

* In a letter published in *The Catholic Reporter,* May 29, 1964, concerning a Catholic prelate's favorable reference to a hoped-for pill which without inhibiting ovulation, would make predictable the time of ovulation, Mrs. Ruether asks: "Is there really such an absolute difference between controlling the generative processes from the side of insemination (as do mechanical devices) or from the side of ovulation?"

The Jesuit weekly review, *America,* has of late printed so many articles and letters on married love—on its problems and affirmations—that a critical woman reader voiced the "suspicion that the magazine's lineage is *Ladies Home Journal* out of *Parents* magazine by the *American Journal of Obstetrics and Gynecology.*"

A second letter-writer in the May 30, 1964 issue of *America* gave it as her opinion that "the kind of concentration on avoiding children to be found in the piece by Father Kane [on the temperature method, May 2, 1964 issue] is exactly what has unleashed the Mrs. Ruethers of this world." But other readers of *America* have approved Father Kane's article as well as the magazine's editorial of March 21, 1964 on "Child Spacing."

The first of *America's* personal experience articles was headlined on the cover of the October 26, 1963 issue with the title "Love, O Love, O Careful Love." In this well-written piece, Mrs. Jane Hanover Adams, who lives in a suburb of a large Midwestern city, flays Catholic magazines which print articles about the whys and hows of family limitation. She fears that such writings may lead her young daughter to question their priest's teaching—that if parents "keep God's law in their marriage they can depend on God to give them the graces they need to fulfill the purpose of their marriage," which is "to conserve the human race."

The author complains that her daughter "can pick up Catholic periodicals around the house, at the doctor's or dentist's office or at church, and find," she suggests satirically, "a ban-the-babies piece by a lay or professional person, or by a priest in sociology or demography, or a survey in which married couples reveal bitterness about their fecundity and the Church's intransigeance; or the afterthoughts of a middle-ager who perhaps took a fling at large-family life during the heady days of the 1940's and 1950's. . . ."

Mrs. Adams would be sorry to have her daughter think that their own small family was "the result of prudent planning";

or that "every couple will produce an excessive number of children unless controlled—when in fact, sterility, complete or partial, is a major medical problem"; or that "babies (after the first four . . .) may somehow be an evil to be avoided instead of a gift to be cherished."

"If there are those," Mrs. Adams concludes, "who would assist us as we try to prepare this girl for her life, if they would earn our gratitude, let them try to apprehend the mysterious making of the family as its natural and supernatural destiny unfolds; reverently study the norms implanted in nature by God; resist all temptations to reduce marriage and family to a mechanical formula acceptable to human wisdom. . . ."

With full credit to the eloquence of "Love, O Love, O Careful Love," some of her readers must surely wonder about the author's acceptance of the Church's teaching on responsible parenthood that has stemmed from Pius XII's affirmation, in 1951, of "the legitimacy of a regulation of offspring." * Mrs. Adams apparently would challenge the teaching of Cardinal Suenens that "the sacred act" of bringing a child into the world is to be "considered before God" and "deliberately determined . . . leaving nothing to chance." † Nor would she agree with the two American theologians, the Jesuit Fathers Ford and Kelly, on "the respective roles of divine providence and human providence in the planning of families"; nor with St. Thomas Aquinas that "the rational creature . . . partakes of a share of divine providence by being provident both for himself and others." ‡

Reliance on God's grace, on divine providence, for the protection of the family was the Church's teaching for centuries. Numbers of parish priests—as evidenced in letters from the laity—still hold to this view. It is reflected in the letter to

* See p. 12.
† See p. 23.
‡ See p. 26.

America, November 23, 1963, in praise of Mrs. Adams' article, written by Msgr. John C. Knott, Director of the Family Life Bureau, National Catholic Welfare Conference. "Mrs. Adams," he writes, "does an excellent job of deflating some of the stock phrases used to express overblown fears. Her major contribution, however, lies in her eloquent restatement of traditional Christian virtues and attitudes. . . .*

A very different reaction to Mrs. Adams' article came from the director of the Diocesan Family Life Bureau in Peoria, Illinois, the Rev. John Dietzen. "It is sad," he writes "that Mrs. Adams set up for herself such a hodge-podge of unChristianity and plain nonsense. . . . The problem she writes of is a real one, but deserves far more factual treatment. . . . Many couples striving to know exactly what it means day by day *for them,* have not found it nearly as black-and-white as Mrs. Adams seems to have made it for herself." [2]

And a woman reader of *America,* living in Toronto, asks, "How much sense would an article like that make to a hungry woman in India with a child at her breast and one in her belly? Or to the starving, the sick, the mothers with handicapped children—all those unable to 'cope,' but who still see the dignity of Christian marriage and possess a love of God. . . ." [3]

Letters from mothers who put their trust in providence—in God's will—sometimes reflect a joyousness, an aptitude for motherhood which makes light of economic hardships. In an exchange of readers' views on the wisdom of family planning printed by the *St. Gerard's Bulletin,* [4] a family tabloid published by the Redemptorist Fathers in Ligouri, Missouri, a mother of four children, aged one to five, recalls her spring wedding day and all that had followed. Their home had been

---

* Yet Msgr. Knott in Dec. 1962, strongly endorsed the expenditure of government funds for an intensive research program in human reproduction which Catholic leaders hope may result in the discovery of a simple, morally acceptable technic of birth regulation (see pp. 168-169).

"a do-it-yourself project from start to finish." "Little did we care that only two rooms and part of the bath had been completed and little did we know that within the next five years we would have enough family to fill seven rooms. . . . Now, I do not want you to think it has all been easy and simple. My husband is a farmer who has to work many days from well before dawn until after dark. I myself work as an R.N. in a doctor's office from 7 p.m. until 12 or 2 a.m. four nights a week. We often say that children are our best crop and friends sometimes kid me about having 'retired' from nursing five and a half years ago. . . . When our four-year-old says she wants a baby girl for Christmas, it is with a full heart that I answer, we will not be having one this Christmas, but if we pray real hard perhaps we will be able to have two next year. . . ."

But another mother of four, married five years, writes in the same issue: "Now I am praying, asking God to please not send us another child for a little while until I get one or two of these children in school. My patience and nerves are worn thin. I do not have much help and find it extremely hard, as do many others I know, to take care of their every physical and emotional need without neglecting my own physical and mental needs. I pray to God I do not lose my mind! . . ."

Health as well as economic problems were the burden of the "Husband and Wife Report"[5] which *America* featured on its cover a month after it had published Mrs. Adams' anti-family-planning views. The article appears in the form of a letter from "John" and "Mary" to a priest friend who is an editor at *America*. John writes:

> According to Mary's instruction in Catholic high-school and college, a woman could have a child every two years without harm to her health. (This being the answer to Margaret Sanger!) Ensuing educational burdens were hardly ever discussed. . . . The idea of having many chil-

dren was given substantial encouragement by friends, both clerical and lay . . .

Mary attempted to nurse each child, with varying degrees of success. At no time did she receive real help or encouragement on breast feeding. As we understand it now, this would have given her natural protection from pregnancy 97 percent of the time . . .

During our early years, we had no idea, or concern about the enormous drain on the mother's vitality that closely successive pregnancies would cause . . .

Even after five children in five years it did not occur to John and Mary that they would "qualify" for the use of rhythm. So when their sixth child had been weaned they resorted to total abstinence for six months. Mary had suffered from varicose veins after the birth of their second child, and after their seventh, developed thrombo-phlebitis which immobilized her in bed for three months. Yet their family doctor did not warn them another pregnancy would be dangerous. They sought spiritual aid from "a zealous, idealistic and intelligent young C.F.M. [Christian Family Movement] chaplain," who viewed rhythm as a "second-rate" means to sanctity and advised John and Mary "to abandon themselves to His [God's] plan for their family." A little later the young couple came upon Cardinal Suenens' book, *Love and Control,* passed it along to the young priest, who after reading it changed his mind and advised John and Mary to practice rhythm.

"Believe me, Father," John concludes, "for a couple aged 35 and 33, the cross of practising rhythm, probably for our remaining productive years, looms very large. . . . There seems to be—among both clergy and laity—a lack of understanding that body and soul will go to Heaven, and that God gave us bodies for a specific and good purpose that we may love Him. . . ."

In her letter, Mary explains that despite their attempt to

practice rhythm after the seventh child, an eighth and ninth had been born. She had "an almost panicky feeling," having heard from many couples that "it hadn't worked for them." "Never having had more than three periods between babies . . . the task loomed up as almost overwhelming," she writes. "Perhaps one reason we and other couples don't have children more *reasonably* spaced is that we are not absolutely convinced of the necessity of staying with the rhythm program." *

After her ninth child, Mary found helpful a book published by the La Leche International Clinic of Franklin Park, Illinois, called *The Womanly Art of Breast Feeding*. By following its instructions she succeeded in nursing her ninth child for 13 months, during which time she did not conceive. This gave her a respite to have a surgeon remove her varicose veins.

From her friends' experiences as well as her own, Mary points out that mothers plagued by "lack of sleep, too frequent pregnancies and crying babies—several in diapers" cannot provide for their children "the emotional calm and peace that induce security." "So many children," she adds, "appear to have suffered emotionally from overwrought parents." Apologizing to their priest friend for being so frank, Mary admits:

> Rhythm is not easy. Every month it is an equally great sacrifice, because it seems our love grows constantly and this is also God's way for us to want to express it. And we know that with Him all things are possible.

Marital burdens similar to Mary's and John's are highlighted in more than a few of the letters printed in the June, 1964 issue of *Jubilee* as a follow-up to Mrs. Ruether's December, 1963 article. Selecting from more than 300 received, *Jubilee* printed thirty-two of them, some at considerable length and

* The Rev. John L. Thomas, S.J., who concedes the unreliabilities of rhythm, particularly for women with irregular cycles, suggests that not all women who claim the method has failed them, have carefully practised it. Cf. report on St. Vincent's Hospital project, pp. 172-173.

most but not all from married persons.* They are material for a sociologist's—or a moral theologian's—note-book, so wide is their range of deeply-felt experience, of convictions about what constitutes a Christian marriage.

Some of the *Jubilee* letter-writers have no quarrel whatsoever with the Church's position. A mother of eight "pleads a case for control in marriage and the consequent value of rhythm as an aid to greater happiness," and finds "ridiculous" Mrs. Ruether's contention that "asking for discipline in sex relations implies sex is evil." A mother of three testifies, "We have successfully used rhythm without strain and tension † ... we Catholic couples—must back up the Church firmly. . . ." Another rejoices in her nine children, who "are beyond all health, all wealth, all ease, all dreaming, reflections of our love kindled from the fire of Eternal Love."

A surely devout, but deeply troubled woman mails her letter from the hospital where she has just born her ninth child, surviving a dangerous hemorrhage. She writes:

"Do you think Christ would abandon me if I use these pills? I don't know how I can raise all these children if I may not go to Holy Communion. And the children would quickly

---

* Complete texts of letters and other contributions to *Jubilee* on the subject will be included in a forthcoming book entitled *Marriage, Love, and Children,* edited by Edward Rice and the monthly's staff. New York: Dial.

† In a letter quoted by Father de Lestapis, p. 176 in his *Family Planning and Modern Problems,* a Frenchwoman who, one would guess, has a regular cycle, testifies that for her rhythm has not only been effective but spiritually rewarding. Having spaced her 6 children as planned, she writes: "After 17 years of married life, we . . . are grateful to periodic continence for having helped us to live our wedded life in a more human and Christian way. . . . We can say with conviction that we really wanted each of our children and that we tried to give them what was best in ourselves at the moment they were conceived. . . . We arranged to make the times when we were doing work which absorbed all our attention coincide with the fertile period. . . . Those who agree to live continently for a few days each month, find far more satisfaction in these relations than those who give way to all their passing whims. Above all, the type of asceticism demanded by periodic continence gives them a far more secure moral strength."

notice and wonder why—they are very perceptive . . . it makes me shaky to think about being pregnant again. And total abstinence is the quickest way I know of to lose my husband. . . ."

A mother of six, confined for the past three months to a mental institution, explains that she is one of the rare women who ovulates twice a month; that she and her husband had been obliged to limit their marital relations to the days of her menstrual period, and that this had taken "a terrible toll on their marriage," such a toll that they had seriously thought of separating.

Still another mother of six writes: "Completely out of obedience to the Church, I follow her teachings, but there are times when I feel like a victim of religious tyranny and times when I have many doubts about my faith. By a supreme effort, plus the help of my husband, I have been able to treat each baby as if it were the first and only child. . . . Our pediatrician marvels at the way each baby is so happy, content and relaxed. For the sake of these six children I am not going to have any more . . .

> My married life has been a nightmare, an endurance contest. Of this I do not complain. Nor do I complain of the lack of sexual harmony caused by the strain of rhythm and abstinence. I do not mind giving up [for the children] nice clothes, new cars, vacations, a fine home, etc. . . . my music, books, piano being sacrificed; or my favorite pleasures—concerts, visits to art museums, lectures . . . (although anyone considering the lack of an intelligent highly cultured society of Catholics may ponder this). I was willing to risk life and health for my faith. I will not risk the welfare of my children. . . . I do complain of a Church that makes impossible demands and backs them up with threats of eternal damnation. . . .

This wife, who is 33, and her husband, 34, have moved into separate rooms, "as an alternative to using birth control or

practising Onanism." "I know I have tried my best," she concludes, "but that is not good enough for the Catholic Church.
I can only hope that God is more understanding. . . ."

A few of the *Jubilee* letter-writers admit they use artificial
contraceptives and no longer go to confession. A woman who
had two children in the first two years of marriage, "began
using the rhythm method scientifically, thermometers, graphs,
etc.," but found from her irregularity "how risky" it was;
turned to contraceptives and in the next six years had three
more children for which she planned. She is doing what she
believes "is right" and yet fears every day that she may go
to Hell—"a terrible doom to consider."

A rancher, graduate of a Catholic college, who has fathered
five children in seven years of marriage, despite his and his
wife's efforts to establish with accuracy the so-called "safe
periods," considers the Church's teaching on marital life and
family size "a bitter joke." He writes:

> The final frozen result of the Catholic Church's so-called
> official position on marital relations and child production
> defies both reason and nature. And conscientious Catholic
> couples are placed on the horns of a dilemma: whether to
> fulfill the vocational vows of marriage calling for physical,
> spiritual, and supernatural union with one's spouse as the
> means chosen to eternal salvation, and thus create the un-
> reasonable situation of producing such a sizeable family
> that can and often does endanger or destroy the physical,
> spiritual, or supernatural well-being of the various mem-
> bers of the family; or the other alternative, to practice
> "heroic virtue" or the complete abstention from the physical
> rights of marriage, and thus to destroy the most funda-
> mental basis for marriage. In short, have we gotten married
> to be unmarried?

The Church's teaching has been similarly challenged in the
letters-column of *Commonweal*. A letter published in the
March 20, 1964 issue comes from an Illinois couple, both grad-

uates of a Catholic university. In giving permission for the republication of their letter they asked that it be made clear that they speak as "individual Catholics questioning a Church position but not attacking the Church."

"Catholic laity," the Illinois couple's letter begins, "talk about Christian marriage. They talk over the phone, in the car-pool, at bridge, to each other, to non-Catholics—but they don't talk for publication. They are aware of the logical indefensibility of their position: to speak the truth as they know it leaves them open to condemnation from within the Church, and the danger of scandalizing outsiders."

Their letter continues:

> To many Catholics—unaware of the subtle differences between infallible dogma and moral-law deductions—questioning the current position of the Church on birth control is akin to questioning the Church. Most Catholic laity do not understand the tortuous arguments from natural law and, if they did understand, would be even more uneasy than they are now. They are forced to give this answer to questions: 'We do it because the Church says so'—all the while feeling uncomfortably akin to the Jehovah's Witness who refuses a blood transfusion.

"Ever since the Church recommended 'rhythm' as an acceptable birth control method," the Illinois couple observe, "there has been a logical dilemma. The end is granted as good—the reverent spacing of children assuring them of human dignity and parents capable of caring for them. The means to this end are the point of contention. . . .

"What has not been adequately understood by the clerical writers on this subject is obvious to the married laity. The sex act is the God-given human means of communicating love, primarily spirtual while physically satisfying. In the sacrament of matrimony two people make a solemn contract to give this communicating gift to each other. Now, to attain a 'good end,' they must choose between their pledged responsibility to each other and their very human family responsibility. They are taught love is the unselfish gift of self and allowed to space children by an act of selfishness. They must withdraw needed comfort from each other for a long period in their married lives. This can tear a marriage apart, ruin love, cause mental breakdown or loss of Faith."

It seems to this couple that "methods such as rectal thermometers, metabolism charts and fertility testers, to name a few of the less repulsive (as well as unreliable) rhythm devices, can be just as unnatural and repellent to human love as artificial barrier devices."

They ask:

> If the end is right, why can't we use means appropriate to the human reason God gave us? Reason is the method man uses to solve his problems—it differentiates him from the animal. Is it right to deny this reason and regard man as an animal subject to the simple desire-release pattern observed in animal sexual acts? Can we be so sure that God does not intend us to use our increasing knowledge of the reproductive system to lead us to the most dignified and effective methods science can give? Can the clerical authorities rightly base natural law on the animal aspect of this beautifully human communicative act?

"Once the theologians grant one particular method to be right," this couple concludes, "the Catholic who feels this method is morally and esthetically repugnant to love has no place to go but his own conscience. Which is where many of them are right now."

The moralists, a psychiatrist who is a father of six, suggests in his letter to *Jubilee,* should recognize "the spiritual, ethical, intellectual, emotional, social and economic factors" affecting different couples. But even if this broadening of view were to come about, it would leave unsettled, he notes, "the more basic issue of the morality of sexuality." Calling it an issue whose study requires the cooperation of clergy and laity, he continues, "Too many statements about sex still reveal the influence of erroneous information and personal prejudice. For example, it is not uncommon to detect the implication that unless stringently controlled, the sexual appetite will be all-consuming, that marital life would be a kind of continuous orgy," that the sex urge is "an animal appetite." The converse of this view "is an undue idealization of the act as "beautiful" or "sublime." "While," he continues, "individual acts of coitus are in fact beautiful in all ways, this is not always the case. . . . There is no other human act which assembles and integrates such a complexity of primitive and sublime impulsions. It is probable that until these and other considerations are duly faced and argued, no solution of the morality of birth control will rest on firm ground." [6]

Six | Illicit—and Licit—
Uses of the Pill

Three years after American investigators had shown that a progesterone-like pill * synthesized from the root of a wild Mexican yam could prevent ovulation as well as alleviate menstrual disturbances, Pope Pius XII took notice of the

---

* The progestin compound functions differently from the oral contraceptive hesperidin, introduced in 1952. Regarding the latter drug, Fathers Ford and Kelly write, at page 339 in their book, *Marriage Questions:* "The drug was phosphorylated hesperidin. After it was taken in prescribed dosages by both husband and wife for ten consecutive days, it was supposed to render the wife's ovum impenetrable by the husband's sperm. This condition would then continue as long as the drug was taken and would disappear shortly after the drug was discontinued. Since the use of hesperidin . . . had no other purpose except to render conception impossible theologians . . . unanimously declared it a contraceptive measure, a form of temporary direct sterilization; therefore intrinsically immoral." It should be added that hesperidin never gained wide acceptability.

sensational development. In an address on September 12, 1958 before the Seventh Hematological Conference, he pronounced the pill licit as therapy but illicit as a birth control measure. With regard to its contraceptive use, Pius XII said:

> . . . a direct and, therefore, illicit sterilization results when ovulation is stopped to protect the uterus and the organism from the consequences of a pregnancy . . .[1]

Pius XII equated the temporary sterilization, or halting of ovulation that is induced by the pill, with the direct sterilization which is effected by surgery, a procedure explicitly condemned by Pius XI in his Encyclical *On Christian Marriage.* There in 1931 the Pope said: "Christian doctrine establishes, and the light of human reason makes it most clear, that private individuals have no other power over the members of their bodies than that which pertains to their natural ends; and they are not free to destroy or mutilate their members, or in any other way render themselves unfit for their natural functions, except when no other provision [as when surgery may be necessary] can be made for the good of the whole body."[2]

After Pius XII, in 1958, had declared that the use of the pill as a contraceptive amounted to direct sterilization, but that its use in medical therapy involved only indirect sterilization, articles began to appear in the theological journals not only on the pill's illicit use but also on its possibly licit uses. The voluminous comment which has since appeared makes it clear that theologians view the progestin compound in a different light from other birth control measures. Mechanical contraceptives, along with Onanism or withdrawal, have been consistently condemned on the ground that they destroy the integrity of the conjugal act.*

---

* There will almost surely be theological objections to the experimental intra-uterine coil which must be inserted by a physician but is designed to be left in place for a period of months. Under a million-and-a-half dollar, privately financed, research program, the inexpensive, spring-like

Recognition of the extensive and intensive theological discussion which has been going on about the pill was implicit in Pope Paul VI's announcement on June 23, 1964 that the Church has under study the "so-called birth control" problem.* After recognizing the "manifold aspects" of the problem, and the "competence" of the spouses, which he termed "preeminent," the Pope continued:

> But the Church must also affirm her [competence], that is to say, that of the law of God, which she interprets, teaches, promotes and defends; and the Church will have to proclaim this law of God in the light of scientific, social and psychological truths which have lately had new and very extensive study and documentation.

"It will be necessary," Paul VI continued, "to look attentively and squarely at this theoretical as well as practical development of the question. And this is what the Church is in fact doing.

"The matter is under study, a study as wide and deep as possible, that is to say, as serious and as honest as it must be in a matter of such importance.

"It is under study, we say, and we hope to finish soon with the help of many and eminent scholars. Indeed we shall quickly give its conclusions in the form which will be considered most adequate to the subject treated and the aim to be achieved." He said further:

> But meanwhile we say frankly that so far we do not have sufficient reason to regard the norms given by Pope Pius XII

---

devices, three made of plastic and one of steel, have so far been tested on 7,000 American women.

A second recent development on the birth control front is the projection of a drug to be given by injection, which would make either husband or wife, or both, allergic to reproductive cells, reported by Dr. Seymour Katch of the University of Colorado School of Medicine (*N.Y. Times,* Apr. 11, 1964).

* See also p. 5.

in this matter as surpassed and therefore not binding; they must therefore be considered valid, at least until we feel in conscience bound to modify them. In a subject of such seriousness it certainly seems that Catholics want to follow a single law, such as the Church authoritatively proposes; and it therefore seems opportune to recommend that no one should, for the time being, take it upon himself to pronounce himself in terms different from the norm in force.[3]

Commenting on the Pope's statement, the editors of *America* observed in their issue of July 11, 1964: "The statement is obviously a 'holding operation.' That is an additional reason why it should be taken as referring, not to the condemnation of contraception in principle, but to the narrower question of whether the use of the pill to suppress ovulation falls into the category of contraception. Some theologians argue—unconvincingly, others think—that such use of the pill is not contraceptive. Of their opinion, the Pope says that he does not have sufficient reason up to now to accept it. Still, he is willing to consider the argument that these theologians put forward. But until he feels obliged in conscience to admit their position as tenable, the norms that Pius XII laid down must be considered as valid and binding." [4]

The norms set by Pius XII in 1958 for the use of the progestin compound were reiterated in this country following the publication in 1963 of Dr. John Rock's book, *The Time Has Come*. Dr. Rock is himself a Roman Catholic and is emeritus professor of gynecology of Harvard University. He had cooperated in the development of the pill. In his book he reports that the compound which he had found from his early experiments could correct sterility in some cases, had also proved to be an effective and safe contraceptive when properly prescribed. He explains that the hormone compound, if taken for 20 successive days during each menstrual cycle, simply halts ovulation during the cycle in question, and that whenever the drug is discontinued ovulation resumes and pregnancy may occur.

Dr. Rock's over-all discussion of the world-wide population problem and birth regulation and of an equitable public policy were commended in influential Catholic quarters. But Church authorities in this country, supported by the diocesan weeklies, unanimously condemned the Boston physician's assertion that use of the pill as a contraceptive is consistent with the natural law. They found invalid Dr. Rock's argument that the progestin pill, unlike "an extraneous device" or "a wholly artificial chemical action" does nothing more than modify "the time sequences in the body's own functions," and that it "merely duplicates" the physiologic action which occurs when human-secreted progesterone acts to prevent ovulation during the pre- and post-menstrual safe period.[5] *

* Dr. Rock explains that the female sex hormone, progesterone, is a chemical secreted by the *corpus luteum* or sac from which the ovum is discharged, this hormone's two main functions being to prepare the lining of the uterus to receive the fertilized egg, and to prevent the endocrine system from triggering the emission from the ovum, during each monthly cycle and throughout pregnancy, of another fertilizable egg. In 1937 investigators found they could suppress monthly ovulation in rabbits by injections of pure progesterone. Wishing to experiment with humans, Drs. Gregory Pincus and M. C. Chang of the Worcester Foundation for Experimental Biology, in Shrewsbury, Mass., started in 1951 to look for a synthetic progesterone-like compound. They ultimately found one that varies only slightly from progesterone in its molecular constituents, in the roots of a wild Mexican yam. In December 1954 the clinical center in Brookline began administering the compound to 50 childless patients in doses of ten to 40 milligrams for 20 successive days of each menstrual cycle; during subsequent months they found that it inhibited ovulation but not menstruation, and that after discontinuance of the drug normal ovulation was resumed, seven of the 50 women becoming pragnant within five months. Subsequently extensive field trials were conducted by Dr. Pincus and Dr. Celso-Ramon Garcia in Puerto Rico and Haiti, as well as by investigators elsewhere, with the cooperation of several thousand women all told. The field trials proved the synthetic compound called progestin to be a sure contraceptive which does not impair the ovaries' normal functioning at a later date. Its medical safety was checked by periodic examinations of each woman volunteer through use of the Papanicolaou smear test, which reveals precancerous cells in the vaginal tract and lining of the uterus, and by blood, kidney, liver, etc. tests. Since the field trials had shown progestin to be

In disputing Dr. Rock, American moral theologians have rested their case on Pope Pius XII's proscription of the pill as a contraceptive, no matter how grave a couple's need to prevent conception. Referring, in his address to the hematologists, to cases of bad heredity, Pius XII made it clear that the pill cannot morally be resorted to by Catholic couples to prevent conception even if one of the parents is the carrier of a dangerous gene. In this connection, Pius XII declared:

> The reaction of some groups of theologians to this state of things is symptomatic and quite alarming. It reveals a deviation of moral judgment, along with an exaggerated haste to revise commonly accepted positions in favor of new techniques. This attitude comes from praiseworthy intention, which in order to help those in difficulty, refuses to exclude too quickly new possibilities of solution. . . .

Correcting those who put forward such views, the Pope continued:

> . . . a principle of morality, correct in itself but badly interpreted, is often cited: "It is licit to correct natural defects." . . . If this principle had an absolute value, eugenics could, without hesitation, use drugs to stop the transmission of a hereditary defect. But it is still necessary to examine the means by which natural defects are corrected and to avoid the violation of other principles of morality. . . .
> On the other hand, to take advantage of natural temporary sterility, as in the Ogino-Knaus method, does not violate the natural law . . .[6]

Pius XII added that when the danger from hereditary fac-

both safe and effective, the Food and Drug Administration approved in May, 1960, the marketing of the first contraceptive pill, Enovid for prescription by physicians for a limited period of years for each woman patient, and in February, 1962, the product of another manufacturer, Ortho-Novum. (Rock, pp. 160-166). As of September, 1964, three other contraceptive pills have been cleared by the FDA. Effective daily dosages, as approved by the agency, now range from five to 2.5 milligrams. (For medical views on the pill's various inhibiting functions see footnote, p. 108.)

tors is serious, a Catholic couple's decision as to whether they should or should not risk having a child can only be made by "the interested party, the doctor, and the specialists they consult." The Pope, however, cautioned: "From the moral point of view it can be said in general that a person has no right to disregard real risks of which one is aware." [7] For couples who face "real risks" the Church teaches that "only one way lies open, that of complete abstinence from any actuation of the natural faculty," as Pius XII explained to the midwives in his 1951 allocution.[8] *

In his speech to the hematologists Pius XII next considered the therapeutic use of the new pill, addressing himself to the question "that is often discussed today among doctors and moralists:

> Is it licit to impede ovulation by pills used to remedy undue reaction of the uterus and the organism, when this medicine, while impeding ovulation, also renders fecundation impossible? Is its use permitted to married women, who, in spite of this temporary sterility, desire to have relations with their husbands?

The Pope's comment:

> The answer depends upon the intention of the person. If a woman takes such medicine, not to prevent conception, but only on the advice of a doctor as a necessary remedy † be-

* Commenting on the objection sometimes raised that for married couples long-term abstinence is impossible, Pius XII in his 1951 allocution, quoted St. Augustine as having written: "God does not command things that are impossible; but when He commands He bids you do what you can and ask help to do what you cannot and He himself helps you so that you can." (*The Clergy Review,* New Series, 36, no. 6, p. 391)

† The progestin compound had been approved in 1957 by the Food and Drug Administration for the treatment of various menstrual disorders and for the prevention of miscarriage. "The compounds," Dr. Rock writes in *The Time Has Come,* "are perhaps effective in dealing with this latter exigency possibly because, by amplifying the influence on the uterus of intrinsic, secreted progesterone, which in such cases may be inadequate, they help to maintain the endometrium [lining of the uterus] in a condition more serviceable to the uterus." (p. 165).

cause of the condition of the uterus or the organism, she produces *indirect* sterilization, which is permitted according to the general principles governing acts with a double effect . . .[9]

After Pius XII had found the therapeutic use of the pill to be licit, theologians turned first to the question of its possible use to regularize the menstrual cycle as a backstop to the rhythm method. On this issue there has been a consensus that under the principle of double effect such a use would be moral—provided a woman's cycle were so irregular as to approach abnormality.

The Jesuit Fathers John D. Ford and Gerald Kelly write in their book, *Marriage Questions:*

When the temporary suppression of ovulation over a period of months is not the precise aim of the treatment, but only a by-product of the total objective, there is at most an *indirect* sterilization; and the serious need of achieving regularity justifies the incidental sterilization in accordance with the principle of totality.

Conceding that some moralists would not approve the pill's use by women whose cycles are not extremely irregular, these authors for their part, consider its use licit for all whose irregularity makes "rhythm more difficult or more uncertain." They state:

Provided the medication itself were not illicit by reason of unjustifiable side-effects or of direct sterilization, we think that physicians may with a good conscience inaugurate treatment with the progestational steroids or other chemicals when the purpose of this treatment is to make the ovulatory cycle approximate average length with regularity, so that periodic continence may be practiced more safely by those who have good reason for practicing it.

Since there is a common assumption among medical writers and physiologists that the 28-30 day cycle is typical or average,

Fathers Ford and Kelly give it as their view that "women who take this as a goal for treatment seem to be acting within their natural right of reasonable stewardship over their bodily members and functions." [10]

The Jesuit authors note that the Rev. John J. Lynch, S.J., at a seminar * held in 1958 by the Catholic Theological Society, expressed the view that "one might judge as abnormal, and hence as legitimate reason for medical intervention, that degree of irregularity which would preclude a reasonably effective use of rhythm; [11] that the Rev. Francis J. Connell, C.Ss.R. writes "everyone has the right to be normal" and finds a couple's use of the pills permissible "provided they have sufficient justification for the use of rhythm;" [12] and that the Rev. Denis O'Callaghan of Ireland judges that "if married persons are entitled to restrict their intercourse to the safe period, they are entitled to make their use of it more effective by any lawful means which respects the natural context of reproduction." [13] †

But Father Connell points out that use of the pill to regularize the cycle has not yet proved "very successful." Concurring, Fathers Ford and Kelly warn against the raising of "false hopes." A procedure they have heard suggested by one physician would be for the doctor to wait until after ovula-

---

* "At the same seminar," Fathers Ford and Kelly recall in a footnote, "the question arose whether use of the new drugs in order to suppress menstruation at the time of an important athletic contest could be permitted, even if it involved suppression of ovulation. We believe that the essential point at issue in this problem is not whether sterilization is direct, but whether there is sufficient reason for permitting the temporary, occasional, indirect sterilization. . . ." (*Marriage Questions*, p. 354)

† An Oct. 20, 1964 *U.P.I.* dispatch from Toronto, Canada, reported that the clergy there permit the use of birth control pills in cases where the control of an irregular menstrual cycle is deemed desirable. The news report read: "The Rev. Frank Stone, head of the Catholic Information Center, said the clergy was not volunteering information about the pills nor telling of the decision unless asked. Limited use of the pills was approved last summer by the Most Rev. Philip F. Pocock, Roman Catholic Archbishop of Toronto. Father Stone said the pills could be taken to regularize the menstrual cycle."

tion has taken place and then put the patient on a 10-day pre-menstrual dosage of the progestin, which would bring about menstruation on a scheduled day—and hopefully—react on the next cycle so that ovulation would occur at a definite, invariable time.

A different medical procedure which has received more attention from moralists, the two authors continue, calls for the standard 20-day dosage of the progestin for three or four months, during which time no ovulation occurs. "The rationale of this treatment would be that the progestin, taken over a period of months, would act as a sort of shock to the entire endocrine mechanism connected with ovulation, so that, when the medications were withdrawn . . . the ovulatory cycle would be balanced and normal."

Whether even this method will work is "very questionable medically," Fathers Ford and Kelly stress.[14] Writing from Belgium, the Rev. Louis Janssens quotes the gynecologist, Dr. J. Ferin, as reporting that "the results so far achieved are not encouraging." [15] *

The confident hope for the development of a new pill which would successfully regularize the cycle without inhibiting ovulation, has been voiced in a number of quarters. In a statement distributed to the Catholic press on Feb. 21, 1964, condemning the use of the progestin pill as a contraceptive, Father Ford spoke of "well-founded hope that medical science will discover soon" such a pill.[16]

The claim that it will regulate the cycle but not impede ovulation has been made for the pill Duphaston, which was approved in 1962 by the Food and Drug Administration as therapy to prevent miscarriage and to correct a variety of menstrual disorders. Manufactured by Philips Roxane, Inc., of

* In the Aug. 8, 1964 issue of *Look,* Jack Star reports that in at least a dozen cities Catholic physicians are prescribing progestins to regularize the cycle. "The results," he writes, "appear promising enough to warrant large-scale tests with rigid controls. Such tests are already being co-ordinated by leading drug companies and research institutions."

Columbus, Ohio, this compound is described as a "retro-progesterone."

"Great hope" for Duphaston was expressed by the Rev. Bernard Häring on his visit to the University of Notre Dame prior to the September conference held there. If this drug "can give an exact fixation and knowledge of the days of ovulation," the German theologian commented,

> then with an abstinence of a mere four or five days, the rhythm method would have the necessary certainty for all couples, and no couple of good will could assert that these sacrifices are beyond the human endurance of faithful Christians.[17]

A second distinguished visitor from Europe, Cardinal Suenens, said at a press conference in Boston on May 7, 1964, when queried about a possible change in the Church's doctrine on birth control, "Naturally, we cannot accept direct sterilization, but I am told that a pill will be available very soon that avoids this." The Cardinal explained that the Church's unchanging doctrine must be applied to a new situation." [18]

The effectiveness of Duphaston as a cycle-regularizer was surveyed in May, 1963 by *The Catholic Reporter* of Kansas City, Missouri. Two Ohio State University professors of medicine reported very encouraging results, but these were not confirmed by other clinicians. In concluding its survey, this diocesan weekly wrote:

> At least for some women under the care of some doctors, Duphaston is useful in regularizing the menstrual cycle, and making it possible to observe the rhythm method. . . .

"If continued use of Duphaston," the weekly commented, "shows that it establishes a predictable pattern of menstruation and ovulation, the implications are great. . . ." [19]

Almost as frequently as they have written about the use of medication to regularize the cycle, the theologians have debated the licitness of a woman's using the anovulatory pill during the lactation period so that after the birth of one child she will not soon conceive again.* This question, Fathers Ford and Kelly point out, cannot be answered "favorably merely by an appeal to the principles of totality and double effect." They see it as one of the cases which "may require a reconsideration of the concept of direct sterilization, at least as it applies to women." [20]

Theologians' arguments pro and con with regard to the lactation period are summarized by the Rev. Richard A Mc-Cormick, S.J., of West Baden College, Indiana, in an article entitled "Anti-Fertility Pills." The affirmative argument, he notes, runs as follows: While nature herself seems to inhibit ovulation during lactation, sometimes the endocrine mechanism fails to function normally. Ovulation during lactation, therefore, is seen as a pathological condition which one may licitly correct. Even though suppression of ovulation during this period would be direct, it could not be called direct sterilization since this presupposes suppression of a normal function.

Medical opinion, Father McCormick notes, "is anything but convincing" as to whether a certain period of lactation is "normally anovulatory." With regard to the natural law, he reports that some theologians believe "direct sterilization is always wrong because direct suppression of the sexual function is not within the dominion of the individual." They make the further point that it would be difficult to establish "a commonly accepted period of normal sterility during the time of lactation."

If suppression of ovulation is allowed during the lactation period, Father McCormick adds, "there will naturally be a desire to suppress ovulation once a woman has reached a specified age because, it will be asserted, at this age a woman is supposed to be sterile.[21]

* If it were assumed that a normal lactation period lasts for nine months, an 18-month interval between pregnancies would be assured.

But Fathers Ford and Kelly put this question: "What if in the future the medical evidence will show that ovulation during lactation really is an anomaly?—perhaps even a pathological one? Would it be permissible then to suppress it so that intercourse during that period would not result in conception? If so, it could hardly be on the theory that such procedure is only an indirect sterilization, but on the theory that it is not a forbidden sterilization at all. In other words, the sterilization which is always forbidden as intrinsically evil would be to deprive a woman directly of *normal* fertility. In some of the writers . . . there is more than a hint that they consider this to be the real meaning of direct sterilization. . . ." [22] *

With regard to the lactation period, Father Häring comments in his article in *The Catholic Reporter:*

> A healthy woman who nurses her child herself acquires thereby a certain natural immunity from the process of ovulation. . . . The Creator Himself provides for the spacing of her child-bearing. But here, too, nature often fails to function as it should, ideally speaking, and moreover the woman may not be in good health at all. Statistical researches in technically advanced countries have shown that even when the mother can and does nurse the child

* "In all these cases," Professor Louis Dupré writes in his book, *Contraception and Catholics:* "one definitely gets the impression that the theologians are breaking away from the isolated act (particularly in its purely material aspect) and more and more tend to see the act in its totality which includes both the intention and the effect. It is precisely for this reason that it has become increasingly difficult clearly to distinguish direct from indirect sterilization. . . . (pp. 56-57)

"Where does the interference with the functioning of nature become arbitrary—and, therefore, evil? Or more concretely, to what extent could progesterone be used for its sterilizing effect if the most essential values of marital love and family unity are at stake. . . . Some moralists would object that in such a case, one would be pursuing the secondary end of marriage to the deliberate exclusion of the primary. But are the two ends of marriage so independent as to allow the dilemma that one cannot be abandoned without seriously harming basic human values and the other cannot be pursued without compromising equally essential values . . ." (pp. 59-60) herself, complete non-ovulation occurs in about 70-80 per cent of cases, leaving 20-30 per cent of mothers with nursing babies who ovulate sometimes and so can become pregnant again. Anyway breast-feeding is simply not possible for a large number of women, for one reason or another, even when nothing would please them more than to do it if it were possible.[23]

Were the pill taken to prevent conception during the lactation period, the supply of iron in the blood could be built up in such cases as Father Janssens of Belgium refers to in his much-discussed monograph. "A normal pregnancy," he notes, "heavily taxes a woman's reserves of this mineral element. When pregnancies follow in rapid succession, these reserves are quickly exhausted, and a lack of iron in the blood brings on multiple disturbances."[24]

A problem similar to the lactation question, Fathers Ford and Kelly suggest, would arise if it is conceded that more than one ovulation during a given cycle is abnormal. "It is said," they note, "that identical twins result from an anomalous division of fertilized ovum at an early stage; and that fraternal twins come from two ova, one of which is presumably supernumerary or anomalous. If drugs were discovered which would prevent these "anomalies" (statistically they are certainly anomalous) would it be permissible to use them, not to prevent conception altogether, but to prevent the conception of twins? This would be a case of reducing abnormal fertility, not of excluding fertility altogether. . . ."

"We have seen," these authors observe, "that according to Catholic teaching the generative act and faculty have a specially inviolable character. Man's dominion over them is quite limited. But just what are these limits? How far does this stewardship allow him to go?" *

* The authors cite the following examples of control of the generative act which some theologians would consider licit [despite Pius XII's condemnation of artificial insemination]: tests for male fertility requiring

Elsewhere in their book, Fathers Ford and Kelly make clear that "the stewardship God has given us over our bodies does not extend" to destroying "directly the integrity of the marriage act" or depriving "directly the procreative faculty of its power of generation of new life." "This would still be true," they explain, "even if procreation were a secondary intrinsic purpose of marriage and of the conjugal act. . . ." [25]

A suggested use of the pill directed in the long run toward ensuring "the integrity of the marriage act" is not discussed by these priests in their book,—its prescription for psycho-therapeutic purposes. In his monograph, Father Janssens writes: "Psychiatrists find that prescription of the anovulatory compound can be valuable in the treatment of certain neuroses such as an obsessive fear of pregnancy." The gynecologist, Dr. J. Ferin, has pointed out—the Belgian priest notes—that "morbid fear of pregnancy and/or childbirth can manifest itself in diverse ways: cardiac difficulties, digestive disturbances, sexual maladjustment (pain in advance of intercourse, frigidity, aversion for the partner)." "Temporary prescription of the oral contraceptive," he observes, "can act as a remedial sedative dissolving panicky fear of pregnancy; once this symptom has been removed, psychotherapy can probe for the deep root of the neurosis and work toward a definitive cure. . . . Far from constituting a direct sterilization, the prescription of progestin [in these cases] helps to reestablish the possibility of a truly human fecundity. . . ." [27]

In a comment on the pill's prescription for psycho-therapeutic purposes, the former President of the Grand Seminary of Malines, Father Anciaux, is quoted in a journal for

the use of a perforated condom which allows some semen to be deposited in the vagina and retains the rest for examination; "assisted" homologous artificial insemination requiring the use of a cervical spoon; and the use of a syringe after intercourse to collect the semen deposited in the vagina so that it may be placed further into the wife's genital tract. The authors note, too, that many moralists would consider moral the taking of sexual depressants with a view to family limitation. (pp. 364-365) the diocesan clergy as follows: "We are of the opinion that this treatment can be justified if the psycho-medical indication is sufficiently serious, even though the distinction between 'direct' and 'indirect' sterilization here becomes extremely delicate. If a treatment with progestational compounds is really only one aspect of a psycho-therapeutic treatment, then, it seems to us, that physician and patient have to judge in conscience whether they consider it a justifiable treatment." [28]

One specific use of the pill as a contraceptive has been approved by a number of Catholic theologians—that is, when a woman is threatened with rape, as were Catholic nuns in the Congo. Noting that it had received queries on this question, the Rome publication, *Studi Cattolici,* published in 1961 the unanimous views of Msgr. Pietro Palazzini, secretary of the Sacred Congregation, Professor Franz Hürth, S.J., of the Pontifical Gregorian University, and Msgr. Ferdinando Lambruschini of the Pontifical Lateran University. In his comment, the latter wrote:

> . . . They [married couples] have at their disposition a more basic means of not having children, that is, abstention from intercourse. . . . The sister and, in general, a woman who is raped, simply does not have the possibility of choosing abstention from sexual relations which are forced upon her in a brutal and humiliating form. In view of this deprivation, the right of directly impeding procreation remains intact.[29]

In this country the Rev. Joseph J. Farraher, S.J., of Alma College, writes that for a woman intending to avoid any act of intercourse but fearing rape, taking contraceptive pills is "legitimate self-defense." "While direct sterilization is involved, the act does not contain the evil for which sterilization and contraception are generally sinful." Father Farraher adds, "Many moralists agree that the use of a diaphragm contraceptive as self-defense against a real danger of forcible rape is justified." [30]

Commenting on the article published by *Studi Cattolici,* the Rev. Francis J. Connell, C.Ss.R., former dean of the School of Sacred Theology at the Catholic University of America, has stressed that the views of the Vatican theologians give "no leeway to the sin of contraception," which is committed when a woman who "voluntarily indulges in the marital act intends directly to prevent the possibility of conception." [31]

Father Connell appears to have left open the question as to whether a woman who is frequently subjected to brutal sexual attacks by a drunken husband may be said to be "voluntarily" indulging in the marital act.

The situation of women in danger of rape "raises further speculation," Fathers Ford and Kelly comment, "as to the extent of man's direct dominion over his reproductive powers." In their view the permissible limits of stewardship cannot be set until theologians agree on the "ultimate reason why contraception is immoral. . . ." "Until such a principle is found and acknowledged," they stress, "there will continue to be discussions of the morality of borderline cases, and about the exact definition of that direct sterilization which is always forbidden."

"Who can say," the Jesuit authors continue, "just what is normal and what is abnormal in the fertility-sterility of women? . . . When we speak of abnormal fertility, do we mean whatever is definitely abnormal statistically, or should we include only what is abnormal in the sense that it is truly pathological in the individual case? A whole series of questions along these lines can be proposed. To arrive at the answers to them means work for moralists and physician alike. Such investigation is difficult."

The answers, they note, "will have to be worked out gradually, with due respect for the guidance of ecclesiastical authority, which in similar matters has intervened in the past (after adequate theological discussion)." As an example of such a discussion and ultimate change in the Church's position, the authors recall "the debates about direct [therapeutic] abortion at the turn of the century."

"The question of the further refinement of the concept of forbidden sterilization," Fathers Ford and Kelly conclude, "is an open one and should remain so until there has been time for adequate theological discussion under the guidance of the Church. For our part we believe it is not impossible that some of the cases we have referred to as future problems will eventually receive a favorable solution. It is not impossible that a re-examination of the concept of direct temporary sterilization in women will lead theologians to admit that the direct suppression of abnormal fertility may sometimes be within the limits of man's stewardship." [32]

The respected German authority, Father Häring, goes further than Fathers Ford and Kelly. At Notre Dame he said:

> . . . if there is a great moral probability of certainty that rhythm does not suffice and that a full expression of conjugal love is almost necessary for a normal married life and even for the unity of the family, then such interference with the functioning of nature by progesterone cannot be considered in every case as arbitrary.

Father Häring raises the question as to whether "such intervention in very difficult cases must be considered as a lesser evil in a moral sense or only in a physical sense.

> In a moral sense this would mean: It is still objectively sinful, but this could be considered as a way out of deeper moral misery into the full light. If followed by those who consider it morally right, we could apply the great principle of Cardinal Newman, "Whoever follows sincerely his conscience, even if the conscience is erroneous, is on the way into the full light" (of truth and virtue). . . .[33]

In their writings on illicit and licit uses of the pill, this country's leading moral theologians have not judged that the progestin compound is safe from every medical aspect, nor have they stressed that it may not be. Fathers Ford and Kelly, however, writing in 1963, point to "the risk of harmful side effects, especially when the drugs are used over long periods of time (as they generally would be when used as contraceptives)." They add: "This, of course, is not our essential reason for objecting to them, but it is a reason too often lightly dismissed by enthusiasts for the oral contraceptives.[34] *

In a brief editorial comment on "The Uses of Pills" *America,* in its issue of January 11, 1964, noted that the French National Society for the Study of Fertility and Sterility, while approving the oral contraceptive because it does not interfere with the sexual relation, has warned against "the possibility of delayed effects, still unknown, of prolonged use." "Even a medical layman," *America* commented, "must wonder whether suppressing a natural function like ovulation for months and years will not react harmfully on the female organism. But there are pills and pills. When medical science designs one to regulate ovulation without suppressing it, the Church's moral theologians may well pronounce a judgment different from their prohibition of the nature-violating contraceptives of the past and present."

The question remains to be answered by the researchers whether any hormonal compound, either one that merely regulates, or one that also inhibits, the generative process, will be free of harmful effects if used over a long period of years.†

---

* In a footnote at p. 345, in their book, *Marriage Questions,* Fathers Ford and Kelly recall that the Rev. John J. Lynch, S.J., wrote in 1960 in *Theological Studies* (Vol. 21, p. 232): "In view of the medical profession's confessed inability even yet to guarantee against seriously detrimental long-range effects of this 'medication,' by what professional ethic does one justify the use of uninformed human subjects in an experiment to which certain doctors in this country on their own testimony would not allow their wives and daughters to submit?"

† For data to date on the medical safety of oral contraceptives, see Appendix.

Seven | Controversy Over
| Morality of the Pill

"Theologian Contends Birth Control Pill Akin to 'Rhythm': Sees Use Within Justified Limits."

The banner headline appeared over a dispatch from Louvain, Belgium, printed February 28, 1964 in the *Catholic Star Herald,* the Camden, N.J. diocesan weekly. The dispatch quoted from the 40-page monograph published in the October-December, 1963 issue of *Ephemerides Theologicae Lovanienses,* written by the Rev. Louis Janssens, Professor of Moral Theology at the Catholic University of Louvain. An accompanying story in the *Star Herald* presented the dissenting views of moral theologians in this country.

The American secular press overlooked the news from Belgium until *Time* reported it on April 10. But the *Star-Herald's* scoop, together with the American theologians' comments, was promptly picked up and distributed by the National Catholic Welfare Conference's *News Service*. There followed, during the first week in March, page-one stories in the diocesan weeklies, some papers running such headlines as "Theologians Debate Morality of Birth Control Pill Pro and Con"; "Battle of the Pill is On: Controversy Waxes Hot"; "Pill Seen Moral for Birth Control"; and "Belgian Theologian Refuted—Defense of 'Pill' Challenged."

The Louvain dispatch based on Father Janssens' article quoted him as saying that "in order to bring a moral judgment to bear upon its [the pill's] use, we should compare it to the practice of periodic continence." Accepting Dr. Rock's theory that the progestin compound merely inhibits ovulation just as the natural hormone progesterone prevents it during pregnancy, the Belgian moralist finds a likeness between the pill and periodic continence in that

> it [the pill] affords a respect for the nature and structure of the conjugal act, fully maintaining the act in its significance in the service of mutual love of the spouses.

Father Janssens points out that when periodic continence is practiced solely to prevent conception, it destroys the meaning of marriage itself. "It goes without saying," he states, "that one can abuse progesterone too with this aim in view."

The Catholic University of Louvain professor takes issue with the theological concept of "direct sterilization" as "any human intervention which has for its primary end the halting of the generative power." If this definition were correct, Father Janssens argues, even periodic continence would be direct sterilization. "Yet," he continues, "it is generally admitted that periodic continence is not an intrinsically evil practice and that, consequently, it has a positive moral value provided that the intention which governs it be good."

Father Janssens notes that the egg which matures and is freed in the course of the menstrual cycle, cannot exercise its reproductive function unless it is fertilized and perishes if not united with a sperm cell. Therefore, he writes,

> periodic continence consists precisely in deliberately suppressing the generative power. In effect, everything is well calculated for determining the fertile period . . . so as to be sure as possible to pose a sterile act.

As have other theologians, Father Janssens recognizes that it is often very difficult for couples practicing the rhythm method to determine the time of ovulation. "If, however," he asserts, "they use progesterone from the start of the phase of the ovarian rest . . . they support the physiological mechanism that tends to lengthen the period of repose; they prevent the perishing of an egg in the course of each cycle . . . and they favor the capability of the woman to conceive in view of the moment when they [the couple] will to procreate anew."

It appears to Father Janssens that

> human intervention is more involved in the practice of periodic continence than in the use of progesterone, and yet no one argues that periodic continence is a direct sterilization or a mutilation.

The Belgian theologian holds that progesterone can be "justified then not only for therapeutic reasons, but by every objective, serious reason; in short, it can be justified in practice by the different reasons which place the control of births at the service of a generous procreation." [1]

In his monograph Father Janssens asserts that the use of mechanical methods to prevent conception "vitiates" the significance of the conjugal act, whereas periodic continence and progesterone do not. "By way of conclusion," he states:

> We would say . . . that one should not have recourse to progesterone when the practice of periodic continence is possible and sufficiently efficacious to assure a voluntary

and generous procreation. One does not employ drugs when their use is not called for. (Still for the sake of truth it should be stated that the best specialists affirm that in the course of eight years of experience no major immediate accidents have been observed and thus the thesis of remote risk is advanced without challenge.) We would also say that the efforts of men of science should be consecrated to an improvement of the method of periodic continence. To this end, two possibilities present themselves: means can be found of launching ovulation at a determined moment in the development of the cycle or—what seems more satis-factory—of finding a sufficiently simple method for deter-mining the moment of ovulation in advance. . . .

"In the cases," Father Janssens continues, "where periodic continence is called for but is not workable or is insufficiently efficacious (for instance, if it is difficult to determine the moment of the recurrence of ovulation in the period following parturition; if the cycles are too irregular; if the temperature curve is illegible; if lack of instruction, above all in the coun-tries in the process of development, constitutes an obstacle to its practice, etc.), it seems to us that it can be replaced by a recourse to progesterone so long as it is used within the frame-work and within the limits of a generous fruitfulness, that is, in the service of a justified regulation of births."

In a foreword to his monograph the Belgian theologian writes:

It is often maintained that moralists' distinctions in regard to acts with multiple effect are no more than the logic-chopping of theoreticians. On the contrary, we take the position that the problem is a very real one, embracing a field as vast as that of all our outward acts. Since we are incarnate spirits, we execute our actions in the material world by the instrumentality of our bodies. . . .[2]

Father Janssens' views on the pill evoked sharp comments from leading moral theologians in this country. A week prior to the publication by the *Star Herald* of its story from Louvain, the N.C.W.C. News Service distributed an article on the illicit use of the pill, written by the Rev. John C. Ford, S.J., Professor of Moral Theology at the Catholic University of America, and co-author, with Father Gerald Kelly, S.J., of *Marriage Questions*. Without mentioning Father Janssens' views, Father Ford declared:

> In discussion of the contraceptive pill one cardinal factor is often omitted. It is a surprising omission: The Holy See has already authoritatively condemned the use of the pill as a contraceptive.

"No new medical factors," Father Ford stressed, "have been made known which make its contraceptive use today morally different from the contraceptive use which Pius XII declared immoral five and one half years ago. Consequently unless and until the Holy See gives its approval to some other teaching (a highly unlikely eventuality), no lesser authority in the Church, and least of all a private theologian, is at liberty to teach a different doctrine, or to free Catholics in practice from their obligation to accept papal teaching. . . .[3]

Queried by the *Star Herald,* the Rev. Francis J. Connell, C.Ss.R., Dean of Religious Communities at the Catholic University of America, and formerly dean of that University's School of Sacred Theology, declared that Father Janssens' position "simply cannot be followed" and that "it is absolutely contrary to the teachings of the Church in this area." He termed the use of the pills for contraceptive purposes "gravely sinful," and said that "Catholics who intend to use them thus must be refused absolution and are ineligible to receive the Holy Eucharist."

From Weston College in Massachusetts the Rev. John J. Lynch, S.J., commented that Father Janssens typifies a school of thought on marriage questions that "is getting out of hand, theologically speaking." Father Lynch said the idea of substituting the use of progesterones for periodic continence was "totally invalid and impossible to reconcile with present accepted theological principles." He added that "it may eventually take a statement by the Holy See to straighten out the whole thing."

One moral theologian queried by the *Star Herald* took a somewhat different position. The Rev. Daniel V. Flynn, head of the department at St. Joseph's Seminary, Yonkers, N.Y., said the Janssens theories, if accepted could mean a "whole re-thinking of the natural law." [4] *

Not long after the debate had started in this country over Father Janssens' views on the pill, clearcut opposition to the traditional position was voiced by an American priest who is a professor of philosophy, if not of moral theology. The Rev. Michael O'Leary, philosophy chairman at Sacred Heart Seminary in Detroit, writing in the March 26, 1964 issue of the *Michigan Catholic,* had this to say of "the bulk of commenting professional theologians":

* In the Summer, 1964 issue of *Theology Digest,* the late Father Gerald Kelly, S.J. challenged Father Janssens' ethical argument. "Father Janssens," he wrote, "is simply not talking the same language as the Popes and other theologians when he argues . . . that periodic continence is a *suppression* of generative power . . . No theologian would deny . . . that there is a positive act of the will on the part of both husband and wife in controlling their sex impulses during the period of abstinence, and something very positive about the practice when it is used constructively for growth in spiritual love and mutual sanctification."

Concurrently, a pamphlet published in July, 1964 by the N.C.W.C. challenged the Janssens-Rock theory that the progestin compound does nothing more than ihibit ovulation. Entitled "The Oral Contraceptives: Their Mode of Action," the 15-page brochure is signed by Dr. Frank J. Ayd, a psychiatrist on the faculties of the Pontifical Gregorian University in Rome and the Rome branch of Loyola University of Chicago. Among other medical authorities, he quotes Dr. C. R. Garcia, of the Worcester Foundation for Experimental Biology, where the pill was developed, as stating that the almost 100-percent effectiveness of the compound "is attributable to inhibition of ovulation, alteration of cervical mucus [so that it is impenetrable to a sperm cell], and perhaps, alhough less likely, by rendering the endometrium [lining of the uterus] unsuitable for nidation [implantation of a fertilized ovum]." Dr. Ayd also quotes Drs. Edward Tyler and Henry J. Olson of the Los Angeles Planned Parenthood Centers

With zealous dedication they spring to the defense of the
absolute sinfulness of any directly contraceptive use of the
anti-ovulant drugs. They emphatically insist that for all
practical purposes the door has been closed to such thinking, and they give as their authority the Pope, who, rendering a decision on the basis of contemporary knowledge and
at a time when, so to speak, the pill was hardly off the
production line, also urged moralists and scientists to give
this matter more consideration and thought.[5]

In a long letter published previously in the March, 1964
issue of *Jubilee* magazine,—a letter which carried the im-
primatur of the Archdiocese of Detroit, Father O'Leary had
noted that "moral complications and difficulties involving the
use of marriage constitute one of the main reasons for people
leaving the Church, for people not entering the Church, and
for people giving up a participation in the sacramental life of
the Church." [6]

In his article in the *Michigan Catholic,* Father O'Leary
commented that the American moral theologians, "after their
recovery from this blow [i.e. publication of Father Janssens'
views] to their absolute position, apparently reassembled their
forces and slammed the door shut with a rugged determination that it will not be open again unless by explicit papal
approbation. . . . One would be tempted to judge that such an
attitude could come only from a person who is dedicated to
non-thought!"

Father O'Leary put this question: "Do the half-dozen
American theologians who say the door is closed really con-

as having written in the April 18, 1959 issue of the *Journal of the A.M.A.*
that the progestin compound does not invariably suppress ovulation, that
it so affects the lining of the uterus as to make implantation "unlikely,"
and so alters the quality of the cervical mucus as "to make it less recep-
tive to spermatazoa." The author of the N.C.W.C. pamphlet concludes
that "the steroid drugs . . . do not produce anovulation consistently,"
and that "their extreme effectiveness" is also attributable to their acting as
"an anti-spermal agent," and their preventing implantation of the fertilized ovum—an effect which is "that of an abortifacient."

stitute the Church or the mind of the Church? If they do, the Church has shrunk considerably since the day of Pentecost."

In Father O'Leary's opinion, the ethics of marriage falls into the domain, not excusively of the moral theologians, "who have been writing absolutely," but also of the moral philosophers since "the subject matter is one of reason, not of revelation."

He pointed out also in his *Michigan Catholic* article that "the European theologians are studying the question," and that "the Dutch bishops (part of the magisterium of the Church, and the theologians are not) say that the door is open."

In the Netherlands, one of the most densely populated countries in the world, a broad-scale debate over the progestin compound began in the spring of 1963. Readers of the American Catholic press learned of this debate almost twelve months later through an Amsterdam dispatch distributed by the N.C.W.C. *News Service* a week after the Janssens article was circulated. In the Netherlands the debate was triggered by the TV speech delivered on March 21, 1963, by Msgr. W. Bekkers, Bishop of 's-Hertogenbosch, and by the Bishop's subsequent article in *Analecta,* the review of his diocesan clergy.

In the latter article Bishop Bekkers does not raise the question, as has the Rev. Bernard Häring of Germany, whether use of the pill to ensure "a full expression of conjugal love," might be "a lesser evil." * The Dutch Bishop, rather, raises the question which Father Janssens answers in the negative, whether the pill can correctly be compared with artificial contraceptives. On this point Bishop Bekkers writes:

> Many sweeping remarks have been made stating the unlawful character of its use for contraceptive purposes. However, most commentators have forgotten, it appears, to ask themselves seriously whether these progestative hormone

* See p. 101.

products really belong to the same category as the more traditional, well-known contraceptives.[7]

In a pronouncement issued August 10, 1963, the Dutch Hierarchy, after noting that "the interpretation of the Divine Law is given to her children by the Church," stated:

> At the very time when so many new views on man, on the meaning of life, the purpose of sex and the notion of love in marriage are being expressed, there has been a remarkable development in biological and biochemical means of regulating and limiting human fertility. The Church is now confronted with conditions which are continually changing. It is impossible to provide one ready-made solution for every problem in a situation which is rapidly evolving.

"The new contraceptive pill," the Dutch bishops' statement continued, "can be no more acceptable as a generally usable solution to the problem of married people than the contraceptive instruments hitherto in use. But moral theologians are discussing whether there are any special circumstances in which the use of these pills could be justified."[8] *

Pro and con views from the Netherlands on the morality of the pill's use were included in the N.C.W.C.'s dispatch of March 13, 1964 and carried by the diocesan weeklies under such headlines as "Holland Makes Crack in Dike on 'Pills'" (*The Catholic Reporter*); "The Pill Rocks the Netherlands" (the *North Central Louisiana Register*); "Debate Over the 'Pill' Rages in Netherlands" (the *Catholic Courier Journal* of Rochester, N.Y.).

In addition to prominent members of the Dutch clergy, leading physicians and the editors of the major Catholic papers in the Netherlands were reported to have entered the

---

* In Hungary and Croatia the clergy have not concerned themselves with the method by which birth prevention is achieved, Father Bernard Häring, C.Ss.R., reports in a footnote in his book, *Ehe in dieser Zeit,* Salzburg: Otto Muller Verlag, 1960, p. 391.

controversy. Quoted as condemning the contraceptive pill was the Rev. Willem J. A. J. Duynstee, C.Ss.R., emeritus professor of law at the University of Nijmegen, who declared that "the use of contraceptives could easily lead to infidelity and divorce." The pill was condemned, too, by the editors of *De Tijd,* a two-city Catholic daily; and by Dr. J. G. H. Holt, prominent sexologist and an internationally known authority on the rhythm method.

On the other side, Dr. C. B. J. B. Trimbos, Utrecht neurologist and psychiatrist, director of the National Catholic Bureau for Mental Public Health, saw the need for "a new and radical approach and an inventive leadership to master the problem of the growing world population." The Rev. Edward Schillebeeckx, O.P., professor of dogmatic theology at the Catholic Universities of Nijmegen and of Louvain, noted "a generally growing opposition to the official viewpoint, even among moral theologians themselves." A second Dutch theologian, the Rev. W. van der Marck, O.P., was quoted as saying that the pill's "actual goodness or badness" depends, as in the practice of the rhythm method, on "the personal attitude and mentality of the married couple." [9]

Father Schillebeeckx's views had been expressed at greater length in a colloquy published in the December 20, 1963 issue of the former Jesuit weekly, *De Linie,* and reprinted in the June 5, 1964 issue of *Commonweal.* In his view "the sexual experience and the possibility of procreation may not be separated in the marriage-*project*." But he points out that "all meanings, *all* human significances of the marriage must not be realized in every separate act," and comments that "this is evident . . . in periodic continence, which has the approval of the Church herself. . . ." Speaking of couples who "want the child, in a human way, with sufficient intervals," Father Schillebeeckx suggests that the morality of the means used will depend upon whether it violates "one's own human dignity and that of the life partner." [10] Father van der Marck, in an article published late in 1963 in *Tijdschrift voor Theologie*,* makes this statement:

> If indeed the two fundamental affirmations which are important in the tradition of the Church are these: 1. the basic willingness to accept sincerely the task of fruitful love and to achieve this task in a reasonable, human manner; 2. the reverence of the person of the other [with regard to] the integrity of the marital act as human symbol-deed, which moreover is full of a sacramental meaning; then it has to be concluded that a birth or fertility regulation by use of hormonal compounds within the intended context and in certain conditions, can be good and perfectly acceptable morally. [11]

Commenting on Father van der Marck's finding the pill licit under certain conditions, but mechanical contraceptives illicit, the Georgetown University philosopher, Dr. Louis Dupré, asks: "What difference can there be between the pill and, for example, a diaphragm, if both are used with the same intention? The fact that anovulants . . . *can also* be used for therapeutic purposes does not affect the moral evaluation of their use for the clear purpose of birth regulation. . . . I can think of no other reason than that mechanical means have been rejected, without qualification, in the encyclical *Casti Connubii,* while the current rejection of anovulants is restricted to their use for the purpose of direct sterilization. . . ." [12]

Across the Channel from the Netherlands, in Great Britain, there has also been lively discussion, chiefly among lay Catholics, about the oral contraceptive and the Church's position in general on birth control. Early in May, 1964, Archbishop Thomas Roberts, formerly of Bombay but now residing in

* Translator not named.

London, touched off a storm when he declared in a Catholic news-letter that if he were an Anglican he would accept the Church of England's view that contraceptives are permissible. A pacifist and supporter of nuclear disarmament, Archbishop Roberts said that while accepting the Church's authority, he himself could not defend the outright condemnation of artificial contraception on grounds of reason. He gave it as his opinion that the whole issue might be subject to "interpretative changes." [13]

Two weeks later the bishops of England and Wales issued a statement which was released by Archbishop John C. Heenan of Westminster. The British bishops explained they could not "remain silent when so many voices are being raised to lead our people astray." They continued:

> The Church knows well that her children are undergoing a period of great strain. Their difficulties are only increased when it is irresponsibly suggested that the [Ecumenical] council may produce a new moral code for married people. . . .
> But, as the Dutch bishops recently declared, the new contraceptive pill now being advertised can be no more acceptable as the answer to the problems of married people than the contraceptive instruments hitherto in use.[14]

After the word "acceptable," the Dutch bishops had used the qualifying phrase, "as a generally usable solution." But in the translation from which the British bishops quoted, this phrase had been inadvertently lost, as *America* reported on May 23.[15]

A number of diocesan weeklies and other Catholic publications printed editorial comments on Father Janssens' views. As a riposte to a letter-writer who found "the 'pill' stories objectionable," the editor of the *Pittsburgh Catholic* wrote, "We fear his appeal is for a head-in-sands attitude, which, however much this may protect 'the laity who are not equipped to evaluate' the issues, will contribute nothing to the formation of thought and opinion on this or any other subject." [16]

The editor of the *Catholic Weekly* editions for Saginaw and Lansing, the Rev. Neil O'Connor, wrote in his editorial column:

> What is involved here is a need of interpretation of statements by Pope Pius XI and Pope Pius XII especially the latter, in regard to birth control. It is a mistake to consider every pronouncement of the Pope as infallible when it might well be only an expression of authentic, authoritative Catholic teaching.
>
> We are not seeking to minimize the teachings of the Church on birth control but we wish to point out that this debate is going on and educated Catholics should be aware of it. . . . [17]

A middle ground was taken by the editor of the *Providence (R.I.) Visitor*. "One thing is certain," he wrote. "Rome has spoken and condemned the pill when used directly for sterilization. This is the judgment by which Catholics must now live. Will this judgment change? It does not appear that it will. However, it is conceivable that new moral insights on the nature of marriage plus a deeper understanding of the entire reproductive process and the pill itself will provide new points of departure for a different moral judgment. . . . [18]

Ave Maria, the Indiana weekly published by the Holy Cross Fathers in Notre Dame, viewed with alarm "the wide publicity" which "Father Janssens' judgment is bound to receive." Its long editorial captioned "Caution Required in Theology Debate," read in part: "Here we are not concerned with the details of the Belgian theologian's arguments. On such a subject, it would be quite dangerous to condense and report a quick translation of his subject. . . . In this editorial our concern is with the Catholic reader's response to the headlines and the news story . . . we know of absolutely no authority in moral theology who would hold that this one article could constitute a solidly probable opinion in this matter. Theologians frequently debate matters of this kind on a professional level of theory without intending their statements to be used in pastoral judgments." Concluding, *Ave Maria* stated: "Catholics must still regard as *immoral* the continuing use of the steroid pills as contraceptives (distinguished from their use to regularize the period or for other therapeutic purposes)." [19]

In his piece in the *Michigan Catholic* of March 26, Father O'Leary, writing as a philosopher, took notice of *Ave Maria's* editorial and asked: "What are the editors concerned with? They are concerned over the problem that some Catholics might follow the position of Father Janssens! It would seem that if this is their problem, the validity or non-validity—the 'details'—of Father Janssens' argument are quite relevant and hardly a matter of no concern."

America, for its part, after *Time* published its story on Father Janssens' scholarly but controversial article, raised the question "whether the theologians can perform their function under the close and continuous scrutiny of the popular press (secular or Catholic)." "A trial balloon," the Jesuit magazine continued, "such as Canon Janssens has sent up may help refine and develop an issue among theologians. But mass publicity calculated to persuade millions of far from dispassionate readers that the Church is about to revise a difficult but clear and firmly held doctrine is something else again. It puts authority in a position where it almost has to act. That hardly serves the cause that Canon Janssens in all sincerity intended to serve." [20]

The lay editors of *Commonweal* commented from a different perspective on the publicizing of Father Janssens' unorthodox views. "What is interesting in this case," the editors wrote, "is the apparent unanimity with which the Janssens position has been rejected in this country. . . . Yet in the area of moral theology, one can never be certain. Part of the difficulty lies in the notorious conservatism of moral theology in comparison with other areas of theology. There seems to be a terrific pressure on moral theologians to shy away from arguing unpopular positions. It is the most conservative voice which rings the loudest, sometimes to the exclusion of newer lines of reasoning and points of development. . . .[21]

The diocesan weekly which broke the Janssens story, the Camden *Catholic Star Herald,* later carried its own editorial comment on the issues raised. In his column "One Small Voice," Msgr. S.J. Adamo, the paper's executive editor, wrote:

> Is it too much to hope that Professor Janssens' views on the 'pill' may one day be the orthodox position? I think such a hope is reasonable, provided the 'pill' proves to be safe medically. I have seen no argument that stands up against Janssens' position except the repeated reference to Pius XII's allocution in 1958. Regarding which I must observe that we make the distinction between infallible teachings of the Pope and other instructions. Why have such a distinction, if we are never going to discuss fallible papal ideas? Is the whole Church a classroom with only one teacher capable of speaking to us, the Pope? Have the Bishops no teaching role to fill? What will we all do if one Pope differs from another? For it has happened, you know.

"In brief," Msgr. J. Adamo concluded, "I believe we owe it to the laity to leave the door wide open on this problem. For if we slam it shut we may wake up tomorrow to find ourselves in a dark, abandoned closet." [22]

"Only *public* exchanges of views can bring . . . clarification," the editors of *The Catholic Reporter,* Kansas City, declared in a column-length editorial of April 3, 1964, in which they explained why they were printing in the same issue a full-page article by the University of Notre Dame sociologist, Dr. William V. D'Antonio, on "Conjugal Love and Responsible Parenthood." * The editorial read in part:

> Too many Catholics still regard the teaching Church as an "answer machine" which produces instantaneous correct responses to complicated moral questions without human effort or puzzlement. A closer acquaintance with the actual process by which moral questions are raised and the answers gradually evolved should be salutary. All Catholics who take part in the process submit themselves willingly to the final judgment of the Church, but while the process is under way they conceive themselves as doing the work of the Church, on the basis of which the final judgment will be made . . .

In commenting on the British bishops' condemnation of the oral contraceptive, *The Catholic Reporter,* in the same issue in which it printed in full the bishops' statement, said editorially: "Aside from the fact that the premature exercise of authority may result in future embarrassment for the whole Church, in the present instance it is clear that further discussion is needed even if the final result is likely to be a reaffirmation of traditional views. For the development of this rationale, debate and discussion are needed." [23]

In Rome, a month before Pope Paul VI announced on June 23, 1964, that the Church has under study the question of birth control, Alfredo Cardinal Ottaviani, Secretary of the Congregation of the Holy Office, the body charged with protecting faith and morals, sharply disapproved "a public exchange of views" on the morality of the oral contraceptive. In his subsequent statement Pope Paul was to say, without specific reference to the pill, that "so far we do not have sufficient reason to regard the norms given by Pope Pius XII as surpassed and therefore not binding." †

Cardinal Ottaviani, in an interview published by the weekly

* See p. 60.
† See pp. 86-87.

news magazine *Vita,* was asked to comment on the statement made in Boston on May 7, 1964, by Cardinal Suenens of Brussels, that scientists are close to perfecting a regularizing pill which would make the rhythm method completely reliable; also on the British bishops' condemnation of the oral contraceptive. "In general," the Cardinal replied, "it is not pleasing to the Holy See that one or another local authority express doctrinal concepts on debated questions, which rather require central direction, since they can display opposing attitudes and a divergence of opinions. . . ."

On the difference between the rhythm method and the contraceptive pill, Cardinal Ottaviani said that the pill "impedes the course of the conjugal act," while in the practice of rhythm "for grave reasons one abstains specifically during periods in which there are the greatest possibilities of conception."

In view of the fact that many Catholics have left the Sacraments because of the Church's strong stand on birth control, the Cardinal was asked whether approval of the pill might not favor a renewal of the religious lives of such Catholics. "It would rather favor," he answered, "the concept of hedonism."

Asked whether the pill would be discussed by the Ecumenical Council in the *schema* on the Church in the Modern World, Cardinal Ottaviani replied:

> Without doubt it is a problem which must be examined by episcopal conferences or certainly by the council if the work of the episcopal conferences is not already definitive. Because of this, it is necessary that individuals abstain from taking positions, from creating confusion, before the problem can be examined by the competent organs.

"The Church has spoken clearly," Cardinal Ottaviani added, "with the encyclicals of the Roman pontiffs even those of recent years. Hence we have the directives. To seek to change the situation simply because of population growth or because there are economic problems cannot be a valid reason in the face of the great doctrinal principles based in great part on natural law. . . ." [24] *

---

* As Vatican II approached discussion of the schema, "The Church in the Modern World," a Rome dispatch to the N.Y. Times of Oct. 20, 1964 reported: "An international group of Catholic laymen of 12 learned professions has petitioned Pope Paul VI and the Ecumenical Council to make a 'far-reaching reappraisal' of the Roman Catholic Church's teachings on birth control. The 182 signatories of the memorandum, from 12 countries in Europe and the Americas, respectfully left determination of the issues to the church. But they argued that the present absolute ban on any chemical or mechanical means for contraception was based on a view of 'natural law' that failed to take sufficient account of modern developments in physical and psychological sciences. It was man's very interference with 'natural law' in such matters as elimination of decimating plagues . . . and in other matters affecting the biological balance, the memorandum said, that had produced the overpopulation problems that made the birth control problem urgent.

"The memorandum suggested also that this implied refusal by the church to consider the problem realistically had made Catholic doctors and scientists 'painfully aware' of a conflict between their professional and religious convictions in dealing with those who consult them.

"The memorandum said that priests also had been 'forced to make a most unfortunate distinction between a formal directive [the absolute ban on artificial birth control means] and its practical application.'

" 'Man's intervention in nature can raise delicate problems,' the memorandum said, 'but he has a norm for their solution in the over-all good of the individual and mankind. It is not a question of denying the absolute sovereignity of God, but of recognizing man's part in the creative process for which God has endowed him with intelligence and will.'

"There were physicians, psychologists, psychiatrists, jurists, philosophers, gynecologists, editors, authors, sociologists, publishers, legislators, educators and lawyers listed as signatories."

The Times' random sampling of signers included Richard J. Blackwell, Associate Professor of Philosophy, St. Louis University; Joseph J. Caulfield, editor-in-chief of the Helicon Press, Baltimore; David L. McManus, Baltimore publisher; Joseph Sullivan, Associate Professor of Psychiatry, Cornell Uniersity; Joseph T. English, Chief Psychologist of the U.S. Peace Corps; Philip J. Scharper, Editor-President of the Religious Education Association, and Dr. John Rock.

Eight | The Priest, the Theologian and the Layman

Searching questions are arising about the doctrinal basis of the Church's teaching on moral methods of birth regulation. These questions challenge an interpretation of the natural law which appears to ignore the human situation of men and women living in an industrialized, urbanized society and they are asked in the 1960's not only by troubled married folk. As already indicated, the editors of Catholic publications, who are growing increasingly articulate in this era of the Second Ecumenical Council, are asking that the laity be included in the dialogue which should precede a re-examination of the Church's traditional position. In their most challenging form, questions are coming in this country from a beginning trickle of Catholic professors of philosophy and of history. Questions are appearing in print too, from individual priests—a new development. They are raised by men of the cloth who must comfort as well as counsel the perplexed and overburdened.

The pastor of St. Brigid's Church in Lexington, Mass., Msgr. George W. Casey, who is also a columnist for the Boston *Pilot,* writes honestly of his dilemma as a priest in *Commonweal's* special issue on "Responsible Parenthood" published June 5, 1964.[1]

"Let's face it," Msgr. Casey writes, "the attitude of the men in the confessionals, hearing in detail the difficulties of complying with the prescriptions of the moral theologians; and the attitude of the pastor in his parlor, talking with honest young couples whom he has known from childhood does vary, with regard to the Catholic teaching on birth control, from that of the scholars who elaborate it."

The priests in the confessionals and parlors, Msgr. Casey points out, "are dealing with people whom they know . . . with whom they are emotionally involved, whose pain is their own pain." To the theologians and the scholars, "a case is a case is a case in the explication of the law, and maybe an opportunity to display their expertise. . . . In practice . . . there is often a conflict between the law and people which moves us in the pastoral ministry to pray for a way out."

The pastor of St. Brigid's recalls the day and hour he decided to modify "the adjectives" he had previously used in his sermons against birth control. It was the day when "without bitterness or self-pity, a man told me that his wife had borne him nine tiny monstrosities in a row, who lived but a few weeks each." He recalled, too, "the case of a poor hapless sort of mother who bore her fifth set of twins in as many years and her husband 'took it on the lam.'"

"At that time," Msgr. Casey records, "such adjectives, with references to those who saw no evil in birth control, as "filthy," "murderous," "animalistic," "sensual," etc. went out of my rhetorical vocabulary. I began to see that family planning was not in all cases sheer wickedness."

It appears to Msgr. Casey that "in our polemical zeal we have over-emphasized the first part of the Canon Law on the purpose of marriage—"procreation"—to the point of "almost obliterating" the second part—"and education of children." "In our day," this priest maintains, "the emphasis on the stated obligations should be balanced. The raising of children should not be left to inclination or natural love, which sometimes fails. The moral imperative needs new stress. The obligation to feed, clothe, shelter, educate and form the children of a family should be given some of the emotional resonance which has hitherto been reserved for breeding. This has not, however, been the thrust and emphasis of our moral teaching or parochial preaching. Even one of the most recent high school catechetical texts contains an example of pious sarcasm in a fictitious Letter to an Unborn Son, in which parental selfishness and self-indulgence are the only possible motives given for family planning."

The wider spacing of children to meet the economic, social and educational stresses of modern life, Msgr. Casey notes, "has traditionally had some taint of guilt attached to it. Agreement with the parents on the part of a confessor or a Catholic family counsellor has usually been given grudgingly and reluctantly. It has been looked upon as a concession to the spirit of the time, the acceptance of a lesser good instead of the greater."

Urging a change in stress in pastoral counselling, Msgr. Casey declares:

> When parents come to the well-considered and conscientious conclusion that they do not have the financial, physical, spiritual and emotional resources to have any more children—or any more for a while—or when confessors and counsellors come to that opinion about a given couple, then they should be made to feel that not only are they to be permitted not to have any more children, but that they have a moral obligation not to have any more . . . rights

of the children already born should be vindicated as well as the right of a duly married couple to unlimited procreation.

Such advice, Msgr. Casey concedes, may seem to the traditionalists "modern and *avant garde* to the point of rashness." Yet he maintains that "the good, religious parents of today measure up to their predecessors in sheer self-control and iron will." "It may be harder for them because they have come up through softer and easier days than their grandparents, and are less used to deprivation. Furthermore, they know better than their elders what stark abstention does to them psychologically. This is not to say that many of the old-time fathers who repaired to the corner saloon for more than one did not know a little elemental psychology too. Today's parents can abstain if they have to, but they are wondering more than the old-timers why they have to. They are not as submissive and content to hear the celibate confessors' routine observation that God has special blessings for the large families, that He knows best and everything will come out right, and besides Canon 1013 says so."

"The Catholic knows that Catholic teaching," Msgr. Casey continues, "is based on the natural law and that there is no going back of it, nor does he insist. But he also knows that this natural law was not written on tablets of stone nor spoken by Christ or the Apostles. . . . It is hard for him to understand why the natural law must remain the only rigid and inflexible thing in an increasingly changing world."

Still another Massachusetts priest was one of seven whose letters appeared in *Jubilee's* June, 1964, collection of readers' comments on issues raised by Mrs. Rosemary Ruether in the magazine's December, 1963, issue. A Boston priest writes:

I am not a theologian but the theologians had either better come up with a better answer or else I and many other priests will not be able to justify our own consciences in the confessional. I ask people to try to observe the law and then I give them absolution. I feel sorry for the people. This is a real problem with parish priests and neither the seminary nor the moralists come close to giving a sufficient answer. One sometimes wonders if they even bother trying.

A California priest writes *Jubilee* that he is "reluctant to face the possibility that the Church could have been allowed by the Holy Spirit to cling so long to an obsolete ethical perspective in the absence of clear revealed dogma." He is inclined to think the solution lies in approval of "the pill" rather than "conventional contraceptives, against which there is so long and strong an ethical tradition." A good case, it seems to him, could be made for "the naturalness of manipulating the fertility of the female, since we now freely manipulate many other bodily rhythms."

A priest who is a college professor in the Midwest notes in his letter to *Jubilee:* "For confessors the greatest problem is absolving the large number of Catholics who confess the use of contraceptives. I am convinced that many Catholics do not bring this up in confession or else they stay away from the sacraments, and even leave the Church."

This professor priest continues, "I accept the current teaching of the Church," but he suggests that there would be no problem if Canon 1013 were changed to read that "the primary end of marriage" is "mutual love and affection." He would see no problem then, since "children are a result of love."

"Since I am a priest," a New Jersey correspondent writes, "I feel that the point of view expressed herein necessitates my sending this letter anonymously. . . . Even in the seminary (the Gregorian University in Rome), I disagreed with the Church's teaching on this topic. . . . It seems to me there are sound arguments on both sides of the question, but compelling arguments on neither side. Artificial birth prevention *may* be a serious violation of God's law. But on the other hand, moral theologians may be mistaken in their interpretation of what God's law is on this question. They have been wrong before. . . . In advising married persons and those preparing for marriage, both in and out of the confessional, I do not act in accordance with my own opinion on the morality of birth control. . . ."

A missionary priest in Africa writes that he finds "the Church's teaching on birth control easy to repeat to others" but he "cannot explain it in a satisfactory way. . . ."

Supporting the Church's traditional position are a college professor priest from California, who comments that "the authority of the Church is located in a context of faith and mystery . . ."; and a Missouri priest who reprimands *Jubilee* for airing "only one side of a problem which is basically not debatable." [2]

As to the debatability of the question, a professor of history at St. Mary's College in Bismarck, N.D., expresses the opposite opinion. In a long personal letter to one of the editors of *Jubilee,* published with his permission in the March, 1964, issue, Professor Eldon M. Talley writes that birth control is "one of the festering sores" which has led him to "feel often that the Church is headed for another Reformation." He stresses that "the vitality of the Church . . . must rest increasingly upon an interior dialogue"; and expresses the opinion that "many of the laity can speak for the Church better than the theologians." "Theology, as something taught," he writes, "has become a tight system of 'becauses' and 'in order thats,' in which its logical coherence seems to have become its chief virtue. . . ." [3] *

From *Commonweal* comes an editor's sweeping challenge

* Professor Talley, who appears to be a follower of the late Teilhard de Chardin, S.J., author of *The Phenomenon of Man* writes: "We have to rediscover, as it were, the Christian message all over again. . . . All we have to do is take off the spectacles we have outgrown. Unfortunately, to take off our spectacles *now* constitutes heresy."

to the Church's moralists. Writing in the magazine's special issue of June 5, 1964 covering various aspects of "Responsible Parenthood," Daniel Callahan, Associate Editor, discusses "Authority and the Theologian." This author of *The Mind of the Catholic Layman* views the struggle going on within the Church over moral methods of family limitation as a drama, but a drama with a plot which the audience finds difficult to follow. "The play is constantly being rewritten, new scenes are added with increasing rapidity, and no one has yet been able to devise a satisfactory ending." Some of the critics, Mr. Callahan observes wryly, see "only an old-fashioned melodrama: faithful Catholics stand firm against the secularist hordes and their Catholic fellow-travellers. Others see it as a court-room drama: the people vs. the minions of the law. . . ."

Mr. Callahan, for his part, believes, "The development of the play to date has gradually uncovered what may be the real and lasting issue at stake:

> how authority in the Church is to be understood, inter-
> preted and developed. For that is the one issue which
> seems most to determine the lines spoken by the actors.
> Whatever he may privately think, the layman is only likely
> to speak those lines which he believes are assigned him in
> the Church. Exactly the same thing can be said of the
> theologian. Now and then, of course, an errant line escapes
> from someone's lips (more today than ever); and some of
> the lines have a double-meaning. Even so, the stage curtain
> of authority hangs over everything: as a source of con-
> fidence for some, anxiety for others, and perhaps as a
> puzzle for most. . . .

The lay editor traces with a fast-moving pen the changes of the past decade or so: "Up until about the middle of the fifties there was a remarkable harmony among the ideals of the magisterium, the theologians and the married laity." The large family was accepted as the norm of a Catholic marriage, even though it was formally recognized that medical, economic or other "indications" could justify, for "serious reasons," recourse to rhythm or abstinence. But these indications "were clearly thought of as exceptions."

In the mid-fifties "social realities" unbalanced "this equilibrium," Mr. Callahan explains. Among the Protestants family limitation had come to be considered a Christian duty. The population explosion began to be noticed. The large Victorian houses were vanishing. The rising cost of housing and of living created problems for families of six, eight or ten children. A college education became important for every child. Wives were now expected to be something more than mothers, husbands something more than bread-winners.

At the same time, Mr. Callahan notes, a revolution within the Church was gathering impetus. "Manual scholasticism" was beginning to give way to "personalism, existentialism"; and "the thought of the Church Fathers began to make more sense and to speak a more meaningful language." "The Bible came into its own . . . as a living source of concepts, perspectives and spiritual animation. It too speaks a different language, a language which makes the old books of moral theology appear dangerously inadequate, if not altogether misleading." "The Second Vatican Council pushed the revolution forward . . . it has cast doubt on many traditional ways of thinking about Catholic doctrine."

> It shattered old certainties. It showed that Catholics could think unthinkable thoughts . . . It brought the beginning of freedom of conscience, not just that old-time Catholic freedom, the freedom of perfect submission to every iota of the law.

While the summoning of the Ecumenical Council stimulated the revolution, "only the barest hint," Mr. Callahan finds, "has shown itself" in its deliberations. "All the while this revolution was in the making, those I will call the 'Center

Party' moral theologians have remained firmly imbedded in the atmosphere of the past."

The birth control question, the *Commonweal* editor observes, is "an unusually troubling one for the theory of authority in the Church." A dialogue between theologians and the laity has been urged as essential. "But what good will that dialogue do," Mr. Callahan asks, "if at the very outset the theologian conceives his task as that of defending, developing and rationalizing an 'irreformable' doctrine?" He continues:

> How can the layman possibly trust the theologian if he suspects that the latter never speaks personally but always as the representative of higher authority? Who delimits the lines uttered by the theologian: his own Christian reason and his informed conscience or those he supports as an obedient, loyal servant? There is just no way of knowing. This is particularly true of published works by moral theologians since one knows that to win publication, they had to run a gauntlet of censors. It is also true, however, of face to face confrontations with theologians. There is nothing more painful than to watch a theologian think twice before he answers a direct question; to listen to him carefully and haltingly frame a precise answer which will not put him or the Church in an embarrassing position; to see him twitch and squirm while defending publicly a position which he (and everyone else) knows to be a weak one, or while devising a jerry-built "answer" to a pointed objection. To bring the pain to a fine point, one need only ask of the theologian: What do *you* think? . . . In extreme cases, he tries to act as if he does not even exist, or as if his mind is perfectly interchangeable with that of the magisterium. I conform; therefore I am. (Unfair? Yes, but not very.)

This sharp critic of the theologians thinks it vital that they understand not just where their predecessors went wrong, but why. "Was it not," Mr. Callahan asks, "a partially false conception of authority which led so many theologians for so many centuries never wholly to reject a tradition which saw any use of sex apart from procreation as dangerous if not sinful? . . . If the theologian sees himself only as a docile servant of an established doctrine, how can he avoid making the kinds of mistakes his predecessors have often made? He must, secondly, therefore explore afresh his relationship to the magisterium, asking himself and the magisterium whether his role has been so conceived as to endanger his integrity."

"It must be possible," Mr. Callahan insists, "for the individual theologian to take, in public, a position counter to that of established teaching if his Catholic conscience and his scholarship so dictate. Otherwise, the layman will never have full confidence in the integrity of the theologian. So, too, the magisterium must allow this liberty to the theologian. Otherwise, it could never have the confidence that he was not simply fawning on authority or that a purported theological consensus was the real one. Finally, the whole atmosphere supporting the enterprise of moral theology must encourage the theologian to be candid with himself, candid with his colleagues, candid with non-theologians, and candid with the magisterium."

The writer sees the birth control question as "above all, a test case for the Church's understanding of itself and especially of its understanding of the development of doctrine. That means it is a test case for the contemporary renewal of the Church." [4]

A year previous to the publication of Mr. Callahan's all-out challenge to the moral theologians, *Commonweal* in an editorial had declared that the moralists should bring to bear on "the deductions drawn from natural law-principles," "the kind of bold, honest speculation and re-evaluation that have been the marks of recent work in biblical, liturgical and dogmatic theology." [5]

This liberal Catholic weekly has published a number of

articles, in addition to Mr. Callahan's, whose authors have called for a dialogue between the moral theologians and the laity. A frequent contributor to the magazine, Michael Novak, author of *The Open Church: Vatican II, Act II,* in an article entitled "Marriage: the Lay Voice," published February 14, 1964, asked that the married layman in the Church be allowed to introduce his experience and insights into the theological discussion of marriage questions. Concurring, John Cogley, formerly a *Commonweal* editor, in a March 13, 1964 article, "In Search of Honesty," asked for a new climate of honesty in the Church and an open-ended dialogue between the professional theologian and the non-professional layman.

It should be noted that Mr. Callahan has expressed honest doubt about the objectivity of both the critics and the defenders of the Church's position on moral methods of family limitation. In an article called "The Quest for Honesty," published in the April 24, 1964 issue of *Commonweal,* he wrote:

> Is it not likely that someone caught in a desperate conflict of family planning would be the most prone to believe that the Church's teaching *could* change? Or that it *must* be wrong? Or that it is all the fault of the celibate clergy? To go to the other extreme, would not the person who honestly believed the Church's position is irreformable be the one most likely to be dishonest about the kinds of difficulties which can *arise* (by shaping facts to fit principles)? It is as if, in both cases, sheer honesty about one side of a problem paves the way for dishonesty about another.

Again, in his reply to a letter from Donald P. Gray, Associate Editor Callahan writes in the May 22 issue of *Commonweal:* "Isn't this almost of the very essence of any complicated moral question: that perfectly genuine and good motivations conflict with one another, that self-deception lurks in every dark alley of ethical decision. . . ." While admitting his "ambiguities," Mr. Callahan does not concede that they could only entail "unconditional surrender at all times to authority." But he agrees with Mr. Gray that "dialogue is designed to lead us into the truth and demands as a preliminary that we speak out honestly, not that we necessarily be right."

The charge that the moral theologians are supercautious in their published studies has been made outside the columns of *Commonweal*. In a footnote to the transcription of his colloquy at the University of Notre Dame, the Rev. Bernard Häring, the noted European moral theologian, says of his colleagues:

> Generally, they are much more advanced in their personal convictions than in publications. This is without doubt a very serious problem. To some extent it is natural and necessary that we all are more cautious when we appear in public than when we discuss these problems only in small groups. This is a sign of respectability and modesty, but it seems to me that the difference between a large public opinion and the publications of moralists is alarming.[6]

"It is regrettable," Dr. Louis Dupré, the Georgetown University philosopher, comments in a footnote in his book, *Contraception and Catholics*, "that at least the technical publications do not reflect some of the doubts concerning the traditional position which are so widespread in theological circles." [7]

The charge that American moralists have lagged behind some of their colleagues in Europe, has been made by Michael Novak in a letter printed in *Commonweal*, April 24, 1964. He notes in a comment on the debate over the pill:

> moral theologians in Northern Europe seem to conceive of their role as one quite different . . . it may fairly be said that European moralists regard themselves as teachers of the Popes and bishops, as those who blaze the trail and go out ahead, 're-thinking the natural law' and also the past statements of the Popes. In one area, at least, an American has conceived his role in that way: Father Mur-

ray, S.J., has shown how and for what reasons the *Syllabus
of Errors* of Pius IX was conditioned by the times. Such
efforts as his have helped make possible *Pacem in Terris*.

The outspoken Father Janssens of Louvain, Belgium, may
be described as one European moral theologian who has attempted "to blaze a trail and go out ahead." After long study,
he laid his conclusions on conjugal morality and the oral
contraceptive before his fellow moralists in the Church, also,
in effect, before the Holy See, the bishops of the world and
other participants in the Ecumenical Council. Significantly,
Cardinal Suenens of Malines-Brussels allowed his subordinate
"liberty of research in order to clarify the problem." The
Cardinal so explained his policy in answer to a question at
his news conference held in Boston May 7, 1964. At the
same time, he indicated to the press that as the leader of his
diocese he does not agree with Father Janssens on the morality
of the oral contraceptive.*

In this country the moral theologians are under fire because,
it is charged, they have not re-examined with open minds, in
the light of a changing world, their interpretation of the
natural law—an interpretation which such leaders as the
Rev. John C. Ford, S.J. and the Rev. Gerald Kelly, S.J. admit
is not clearly based on revelation; † and because they insist
the Church's teaching on conjugal morality and birth control
is unchangeable even though it has never been made the
subject of an infallible Papal pronouncement.‡

As a philosopher, Dr. Louis Dupré finds unacceptable the
reasoning of the Rev. J. S. Fuchs, S.J., who is quoted by
Fathers Ford and Kelly to the effect that the doctrine set
forth by Pius XI in *Casti Connubii,* while not infallibly proposed, was in the form of such a solemn declaration that

---

* See p. 94.
† See p. 37.
‡ The Pope's power to promulgate infallible doctrine was affirmed by
the First Vatican Council in 1870.

"one who is unwilling to admit it sins against the faith but is not a heretic." Dr. Dupré finds no more acceptable the assumption of Fathers Ford and Kelly that the doctrine is "irrevocable" because it is "very likely already taught infallibly *ex iugi magisterio*," that is to say, that it is being taught by all the bishops of the world.

The two Jesuit scholars' reasoning is as follows:

> a doctrine not yet infallibly defined or clearly proposed as infallible may be so much a part of the Church's teaching that it does exclude all possibility of error. That it has not yet been infallibly proposed may be owing to extrinsic factors, for instance, to the fact that there was no need to define what nobody denied. Or there might simply be a case in which the doctrine is actually being taught *ex iugi magisterio*.

Fathers Ford and Kelly recall that "when the *vota* of the bishops of the world on the doctrine of the Assumption were gathered, it was found that the doctrine was already *de fide ex iugi magisterio*." * "A similar survey," the Jesuit scholars suggest, "of the teaching of the universal Church about contraception might reveal that this doctrine too is already being infallibly proposed *ex iugi magisterio*. We are convinced that the survey would show this and that it would have done so even before *Casti Connubii*. . . ." [8]

The simple fact, Dr. Dupré comments, "is that such an official survey was never made."

In Dr. Dupré's view, "there is nothing between infallible and fallible." But he adds, ". . . the non-infallible character of the proposed doctrine by no means implies that it is not true, nor that the Church will eventually alter its basic stance." He does not expect this to happen, chiefly because

---

* The dogma of the Assumption, the bodily taking up into heaven of the Virgin Mary after her death, was proclaimed *ex cathedra*, as infallible doctrine, by Pope Pius XII on Nov. 1, 1950.

the Church's *basic* teachings on the ends of marriage and
of the marriage act are so obviously sound that only the
utmost confusion in the justification of, and practical deductions from, these teachings could open them to honest
doubt.

What will happen, the Georgetown philosopher anticipates,
"is that the very complexity of the cases proposed to today's
moral theologians, as well as their own growing awareness
of the problems involved, will compel the experts to take a
more sophisticated attitude both towards the articulation in
moral principles of the Church's basic teaching and towards
their application." [9]

Dr. Dupré points out that in the past the Church has
changed its position "on important issues of the moral law
in cases where there is no indisputable scriptural evidence of
a positive divine law to the contrary." *

As have other Catholic writers, he cites as a familiar case in
point the Church's ultimate reversal of its prohibition against
lending money at interest.[10]

"In former ages," the Rev. Bernard Häring, C.Ss.R. observed
in his colloquy at the University of Notre Dame,

the Church forbade absolutely the taking of interest on
capital. *The Council of Vienne* (1311-1312) declared in a

---

* A recent case in point is the mitigation by the Holy Office of the
penalties for cremation, reported in a Rome dispatch distributed May 15,
1964 by the *News Service of the National Catholic Welfare Conference.*
The dispatch reads in part: "Competent sources in the Vatican said an
instruction has been sent to the bishops of the world on the subject of
cremation, but that it was not designed as a wholesale authorization to
substitute cremation for the traditional form of Christian interment or
burial. It was pointed out that the Church has always held that the bodies
of deceased Catholics be interred. This is in accordance with ancient
Christian practices, it was stated, and is also more in accordance with
the doctrine of the resurrection of the body at the Last Judgment. It was
also noted in the instruction that cremation objectively speaking is not
contrary to faith. . . . It was pointed out that the anti-religious aspect in
cremation is nowadays less violent. In some places and under certain
circumstances, it is required either by national custom or by serious
reasons of a hygienic or economic nature. . . ."

decree (not in a doctrinal constitution): "If one would fall into the error to assert that one could lend money for interest without sinning, then it is our decision that he has to be treated as a heretic, and we give the order to the bishops and to the inquisitors to proceed with the greatest severity against those who are suspected of having fallen into this error."

Capital in earlier times was not fruitful and was lent only to those who were in distress, Father Häring explains. To demand interest from them would have been the same as to misuse the need of a neighbor for the selfish enrichment of those who were in better economic situations. . . . Capital in a dynamic economy is by its nature, or, rather by the whole of the economic structure, fruitful. While it is justifiable to demand a moderate rate of interest from those to whom one lends his capital, it remains still true that nobody is allowed to misuse the painful situation of the poor for his own profit. . . ."

It was not until 1931, Father Häring notes, that Pius XI, in the encyclical *Quadragesimo Anno,* stressed the right to interest on capital.[11] *

"The general principle of justice," Dr. Dupré comments, "remains true today as it was in a precapitalist society . . . The same can be said about the basic precepts of the natural law regarding chastity and procreation in marriage. But these precepts have to be specified in their concrete applications, and the applications may change as man himself changes." [12]

The whole issue, in the view of this Catholic professor, "has become obfuscated by the fact that too many people

* Father Thomas comments: "The question of taking interest on money lent for investment was practically settled after Lessius *et al* clarified the nature of modern economic enterprises and reasonable interest rates. The more or less academic debate dealt with by Pius XI in *Quadragesimo Anno* had to do with an argument growing out of Leo XIII's encyclical *Rerum Novarum,* of 1891."

forget that authentic *human* love cannot be attained without self-control."

From a perspective not unlike that of the psychiatrist * quoted in *Jubilee,* Dr. Dupré observes:

> The marriage act is undoubtedly of great value and in some cases it may be essential to the survival of marital love. But to consider it as an absolute value to be pursued even at the expense of all others is to isolate it from the totality of existence. Such a view would conflict more with the total finality of man than the one . . . criticized. . . . Indeed, from [the] position advanced . . . it follows that *ideally,* that is, whenever the essence of marriage is not jeopardized, continence (either periodic or prolonged) remains *the* solution for a married couple unable to provide for more children, since in continence alone no major value is being sacrificed—always supposing that neither marital love nor the education of the children suffer from it.

It seems to him that "our psychologizing generation is all too easily inclined to consider the tension which may result from continence as the supreme evil in life, and to forget that it might lead to a deepening of affection. . . ."

Yet Dr. Dupré realistically recognizes that "not every couple is able to attain the highest level of spiritual love, certainly not at once." He stresses that allowance must be made for growth and development in man's moral and spiritual life, as in his physical. "We readily admit," he writes, "that *ideally* the highest perfection would consist in having the marriage act with all of its consequences or in not having it at all, when those consequences cannot be accepted. But we wonder whether this ideal is always an essential perfection which man cannot omit without violating the moral law. If it is not, then we can only conclude that *le mieux est parfois l'ennemi du bien* [the best is sometimes the enemy of

* See pp. 82-83.

the good], and that someone should not be called immoral because he has not reached the heights of perfection."

In his proposed formulation, Dr. Dupré goes a shade further than Father Häring, who suggests that the use of the oral contraceptive might be considered a lesser moral evil in cases where "a full expression of conjugal love is almost necessary for a normal married life and even for the unity of the family." *

"Christianity is a difficult religion," Dr. Dupré points out, "but it is not simplistic. It has probably set up a higher moral code than any ethical system in all the ages. But at the same time, it has always taken a starkly realistic view of human nature and its limitations. It was founded on the Cross and cannot be practiced outside the law of the Cross. But it is also a religion based on the Resurrection; it is solicitous of life and love. . . ."

"For a Catholic," he concludes, "arguments alone are insufficient in matters where the Church has chosen to lead the faithful; the final answer must come from the Church.

> But we think that this answer has not yet been given, and that ultimately it might vary somewhat from what moral theologians teach publicly today; not because of a basic change in stance, but because of increasing insight into the complexities of the problem.

Any modification of the Church's position, Dr. Dupré concludes, "will not make things easier for the Christian. Instead of living by a universal and well-defined precept, he would have to return to his own conscience and decide, in his full responsibility before God, how he must respond to his vocation to create in Christ." [13]

---

* See p. 101.

Only two states still have anti-birth control laws that are
anything but dead letters. A Massachusetts statute bans the
dissemination of printed information about fertility limitation
and has been so construed as to prohibit the operation of
privately sponsored birth control clinics. A Connecticut anti-
obscenity law goes further and makes it a crime not only for
doctors to prescribe but for individuals to use "drugs or instruments to prevent conception." Both laws were passed in
the latter part of the 19th century, not at the behest of the
Catholic Church but of Anthony Comstock, the celebrated
vice crusader, and of Protestants of his Puritan persuasion.
But the Catholics have blocked all attempts in this century
to repeal or modify these laws.

Today a growing number of Catholic thinkers are declaring
that in a pluralistic society such as ours the Church should

not attempt to impose its moral precepts on others not of their faith. Their position may surprise and please non-Catholics.

The late Rev. Gustav Weigel, S.J., of Woodstock College, wrote in 1960:

> God's law may forbid this or that action, but the state may wisely permit it lest greater evil fall upon the community. . . . The function of civil law is not to teach theology or even the moral views of the legislator. . . . The morality of divorce, birth-control, liquor traffic and the like are one thing. Civil legislation about them is quite another.[1]

From the University of Notre Dame, Father O'Brien, wrote in his *Look* magazine article in 1961:

> An action once universally condemned by Christian churches and forbidden by the civil law is now not only approved by the overwhelming majority of Protestant denominations, but also, deemed, at certain times, to be a positive *religious duty*. This viewpoint has now been translated into action by the majority of people in this country. Repeated polls have disclosed that most married couples are now using contraceptives in the practice of birth control.

"To try to oppose the general religious and moral conviction of such a majority by a legislative fiat," Father O'Brien continued, "would be to invite the same breakdown of law and order that was occasioned by the ill-starred Prohibition experiment."

"Conscience and religion," Father O'Brien reasons, "are concerned with private *sin*: the civil law is concerned with public *crimes*." [2]

In the case of Prohibition it was, of course, the Protestant churches—although not all—which tried to impose their moral views on society in general.

With reference to the Connecticut law, the Rev. John

Courtney Murray, S.J., of Woodstock College, Maryland, observes bluntly:

> Since it makes a public crime out of a private sin, and confuses morality with legality, and is unenforceable without police invasion of the bedroom, the statute is indefensible as a law. . . .[3]

Commenting on both the Connecticut and Massachusetts laws, the Rev. John J. Lynch, S.J., Professor of Moral Theology at Weston College, Connecticut, writes:

> Except perhaps to forestall the establishment of public birth control clinics . . . the law has proved meaningless in practical effect. Substantially unenforced and unenforceable, it has become in latter years a periodic source of bitter religious animosity. . . . To regret that the prohibition was ever incorporated into civil statute would seem altogether consonant with our juridic principles which determine the essential properties of good law.

But Father Lynch points to a difficulty: if the Church were to withdraw its opposition to repeal or modification of the civil law—or even if it simply ignored the issue—the general public might conclude it was taking "a relaxed attitude toward the moral law." "Perhaps," Father Lynch concludes, "the difficulty is not insurmountable, but it does appear to be considerable." [4]

James O'Gara, managing editor of *Commonweal,* gives his own explanation of the Catholic opposition to repeal of unenforceable laws in the two states:

> Catholics in New England had their noses rubbed in the dirt by Yankee Protestants for a long, long time. . . . As a result, they now enjoy being in a position to say "No"—on something like the birth control laws—too much to give it up. But this, of course, is explanation, not justification.

Mr. O'Gara asks, "How long are the rest of us supposed

to suffer?" while waiting for an end to "the traditional hostility . . . between Brahmin and Catholic?" He writes that he cannot "remember participating in any public meeting with a free-and-open question period" in which he as a Catholic was not challenged on the Massachusetts and Connecticut laws.[5]

One answer Mr. O'Gara is able to give the Church's critics is that even though Catholics have opposed repeal of the Massachusetts and Connecticut laws, they "have never introduced similar legislation, even in areas where their numbers are great." But he is frank in stating that since there is no popular consensus to support the legal ban on distribution of contraceptives to married couples, such laws are not only unenforceable but "tend to lead to contempt for all law."

Speaking for himself, Mr. O'Gara believes "it is quite possible to drop our opposition to . . . repeal, while still making clear that the Church continues to forbid artificial birth control." At the same time, Mr. O'Gara suggests it would be "good public policy to restrict the sale of birth control devices to the married" through legislation forbidding the advertising of contraceptives and their sale through such means as slot machines.[6]

As to repeal of the two New England laws, the Rev. John Maguire, C.S.C. takes the same position as Mr. O'Gara. He writes:

> . . . we feel that a Catholic can justifiably favor repeal of the Connecticut and Massachusetts anti-contraceptive laws, or breathe happily if they are declared unconstitutional. But since this is a prudential judgment not every Catholic would agree.[7]

In Connecticut the Church has not to date relaxed its opposition to any change in the law. But in Massachusetts, Cardinal Cushing said early in 1963 on television, "I have no right to impose my thinking which is rooted in religious thought, on those who do not think as I do." He added that if the Massachusetts law should come up for legislative review, he would "confer with the best authorities we have to find out how I am obligated in the matter." The action he intends, he said, "is just to explain our position, and not go on campaigning." [8]

The Rev. Henry V. Sattler, assistant director of the National Catholic Welfare Conference's Family Life Bureau is of the opinion that:

> the Catholic Church and its members, following their civic duty, must of course insist upon the right to *propose* their own views and to *oppose* positions they hold to be wrong, but never to *impose* their own moral doctrines upon individuals who do not accept the Catholic teaching.[9]

In quite a different category from unenforceable state laws against birth control is the use of public monies for contraceptive services. In various states and cities, Catholics have exercised their political power to prevent public hospitals and welfare departments from supplying such services. Yet today, in New York City, seven municipal hospitals are conducting contraceptive clinics.

Previous to 1958 an unwritten regulation of the New York City Department of Hospitals had prohibited staff physicians from providing contraceptive services in any of its fourteen general hospitals, where approximately 27,000 babies are delivered every year. The unwritten ban took no account of a woman's own religious belief or personal preference. It was rigidly imposed despite the state law, which clearly permits physicians to give birth control information; despite, too, the New York Academy of Medicine's view that hospitals are the proper place for birth control clinics. There appeared to be no hope of a change in policy until a series of articles was published by the *New York Post* in 1957. During the public debate which ensued, the Archdiocese of New York stoutly opposed letting down the bars. Other Catholic voices, however, were heard. James Finn, then Associate Editor of the *Commonweal,* wrote in part:

> Other citizens cannot expect Catholics to change their beliefs to conform to this newer consensus. But neither can Catholics expect to control the beliefs and practices of others. . . . If in this controversy Catholics were to rely on education, personal moral suasion, and indoctrination rather than on a civil directive which embitters and alienates many people, the Church would surely gain in the long run.

Catholics, the *Commonweal* editor noted, had been "acting on a principle and asserting their concern about the way in which their taxes are spent." He noted, too, that "the continuing efforts of Protestant groups to ban bingo in New York afforded an example of a group attempting to impose upon the total social body what it believes to be right." Urging a policy of self-limitation on all groups, Mr. Finn wrote:

> It is practical wisdom for Catholics—or anyone else, not to attempt to have laws erected or directives established in accordance with their beliefs except where there is good reason to believe that there is a consensus; only, that is, where the society can sustain such laws. . . .[10]

The decision finally reached by the New York City Board of Hospitals took into account the views of both sides. It directed the municipal hospitals to provide contraceptive services to patients whose "life and health in the opinion of the medical staff may be jeopardized by pregnancy and who wish to avail themselves of such services." It also directed that "physicians, nurses and other hospital personnel who have religious or moral objections should be excused from participation in contraceptive procedures."

Father O'Brien saw in the New York City decision a sign of "some progress." "It would be well," he commented, "to settle the policy of public hospitals and health agencies . . . in a conference of local Protestant, Catholic and Jewish spokesmen." The objective would be "to respect the rights of con science of all concerned." [11]

As a result of the policy adopted by the Board of Hospitals in September, 1958, contraceptive clinics were in operation by September, 1964 in twelve of New York City's fifteen municipal hospitals, with three more in prospect. Since questions had been raised by some staff physicians as to the precise nature of medical indications, the Department in May, 1964 distributed as information to its physicians a statement from the New York Academy of Medicine which sets down three guide-lines for the prescription of contraceptive services. The first is that "the primary responsibility for judging rests with the attending physician"; the second, that "the health of the potential mother is the primary and paramount consideration and criterion"; and the third, that attending physicians should adopt the World Health Organization's definition of health as being "a state of complete physical, mental and social well-being and not merely the absence of disease or infirmity." In a subsequent talk with the press on July 13 the Commissioner of Hospitals stressed that the distribution of the Academy's guide-lines marked no change in the Board of Hospital's policy as agreed upon in 1958.[12]

In New York City's Department of Welfare, the official anti-birth control policy prevailed until January, 1964. It was then announced that married women on relief living with their legal spouses would be given, if they so requested and if the case-worker had no contrary religious convictions, a list of municipal and voluntary hospitals which conduct birth control clinics and Catholic institutions which have opened family planning or rhythm clinics; and that the Department would reimburse for clinic services found to be medically necessary.[13] Six months later, Welfare Commissioner James E. Dumpson announced on a radio program a change in procedure, under which a case-worker who has moral scruples against the practice of birth control will be required to refer to his or her supervisor a client's request for such services. The Commissioner said, too, that he expected soon to mail to eligible relief clients an announcement that they might request such services. Mr. Dumpson explained that although as a Roman Catholic he opposes contraception, he believes it to be his duty "in a pluralistic society" to assist those who seek help.[14] It has been the Department's policy, he said later, to reimburse for services given whenever the physician, on his own responsibility, finds them medically necessary.[15]

An over-all policy on the provision of birth control services, identical with that of the New York City Department of Welfare, was announced by the State Board of Social Welfare, also in January, 1964.[16] In both City and State women relief clients not living with legal spouses—a group which constitutes four-fifths of the heads of relief families—may not be referred for birth control services.

In Illinois, the State Public Aid Commission made no mention of marital status when it authorized in December, 1962, the use of public funds for birth control services and supplies to be provided to recipients of public assistance. But the Commission's move aroused strong Catholic opposition. The Legislature stepped in, and through its powers of appropriation limited the provision of such services to relief clients living with legal spouses. In 1963 the Legislature set up an *ad hoc* commission to hold hearings and recommend laws on birth control to the 1965 General Assembly.

In the nation's capital, a pilot birth control project was inaugurated in April, 1964, by the District Health Director. In the clinic conducted by the District of Columbia's General Hospital and at five of the Department of Health's local centers, free birth control services and supplies, or as an alternative, instruction in the rhythm method, will be offered women newly delivered of a child and those eligible for aid to dependent children. The modest starting annual budget, provided by Congressional appropriation, is expected to care for 2,500 women.[17] Commenting on the tax-supported program, Bishop Philip M. Hannan of the Archdiocese said it contains elements which are "morally repugnant" to many citizens, but he noted that participation in the program is entirely voluntary. The Bishop announced that the Archdiocese was about to open its own rhythm clinics.[18]

On the West Coast, the San Francisco General Hospital initiated in May, 1964 a voluntary birth control service, using for the first year a $10,840 private donation. The item had originally been inserted in the Health Department's budget but was vetoed by the Mayor as involving "a highly controversial program." When the private gift was offered, the Board of Supervisors agreed to accept it on the recommendation of the San Francisco Medical Society. Family planning services are to be provided to indigent mothers delivered at the city hospital.[19]

Since 1960, in New Jersey, public health agencies have been allowed to refer mothers on request to Planned Parenthood Centers. The same referral plan is followed by the State Welfare Department. And in Maryland, since 1962, caseworkers for the State Board of Welfare have referred relief recipients for family planning services when they deem it advisable. In March, 1964, the Archbishop of Baltimore requested that individual caseworkers be excused from from making referrals which "conflict with his or her religious moral convictions." His request was denied by the acting chairman of the Board of Welfare, who stated that the referral policy "requires all caseworkers in local departments to take the necessary action when referral is indicated." [20]

Two issues are implicit in the provision of birth control services to relief recipients, *Commonweal's* Mr. O'Gara points out:

> There are people who have ten or twelve children one after another while subsisting on welfare, simply because

they know no way of preventing or spacing births. This does not necessarily promote human dignity or protect the welfare of the children involved.

Yet the other side of the picture is not attractive. How free is a family on welfare if a case-worker "suggests" that it has enough children and that the services of a birth control agency be sought? No matter how careful social workers might try to be in such a situation, the suggestion of coercion or terminated benefits would be bound to rise in the background. . . .

Mr. O'Gara thinks a possible solution "is for the government to stay out of the family planning picture entirely, but for the churches and voluntary agencies to make yeoman efforts to see that welfare families really do have freedom of choice." He argues, "Let those who believe in artificial birth control operate their clinics; let Catholics in turn intensify their efforts to perfect the rhythm system and set up their clinics. In this way every man could follow his conscience, and we would keep government out of this very sensitive area. . . ." [21]

In a number of states over the country, contraceptive services are provided by public health agencies assisted by federal funds—a policy initiated in 1942 during the tenure of Surgeon General Thomas Parran, a Catholic. Commenting, during the 1960 campaign, John F. Kennedy, who was to become the country's first Catholic president, said:

Apparently Surgeon General Parran felt that one's private beliefs and practices did not justify any use of public office to interfere with the private beliefs and practices of others. I wholeheartedly share that belief—indeed, under our wise system of separating church and state, there can be no other conclusion. [22]

Some leading Catholic laymen are today taking a "live-and-let live" position, as shown by a Planned Parenthood Federation poll. It was conducted in the fall of 1960 during the lively debate over electing a Catholic to the Presidency. A Statement on Religious Liberty signed by 166 Roman Catholic laymen had appeared on October 6th. The next day the PPF wired each signer asking two questions:

> (1) Would you agree that non-Catholic doctors and laymen should have equal freedom of conscience and action concerning birth control?
>
> (2) Would you agree that public officials should respect such freedom of religious belief in policies affecting medical institutions?

As many as 79, or almost half of the 166 Catholic laymen, sent replies. Their responses broke down as follows:

> 47 (59 percent of respondents; 28 percent of those queried) replied yes to (1)
>
> 40 (51 percent of respondents; 24 percent of the total) replied yes to (2)
>
> 11 (14 percent of respondents; 7 percent of the total), while not answering either question, said they strongly opposed such laws as those in Connecticut and Massachusetts.
>
> 7 sent unclassifiable answers.
>
> 12 made no comment on either question or else referred PPF to the Statement on Religious Liberty.

All of the 79 laymen who replied vigorously supported their Church's position on contraception. The following joint reply was received from 26 laymen, including a number of Catholic educators and editors:

> We in the first place affirm our belief in the Catholic Church's teaching that birth prevention by chemical or mechanical means is immoral, even though we recognize that many other Americans in good faith believe otherwise. Secondly, we affirm our belief that the state has no competence to legislate private conviction or conduct on birth

control and that non-Catholic doctors and laymen should therefore be guaranteed full freedom of conscience in this matter as a civil right. Thirdly, we affirm our belief that since public officials have no competence to legislate private conduct in this matter, public authorities should respect the civil right of individual citizens to determine their own conscience and conduct in policies affecting birth control in governmentally operated medical institutions. In this area public authorities should neither prohibit nor impose birth control. Fourthly, we affirm our belief that privately operated medical institutions, even when they receive supplementary aid from public funds, have the right to determine their policies on birth control in the light of their own conscientious convictions. Lastly, we affirm our belief that the rights of conscience should not be confused in this matter by urging the use of public funds to promote governmentally sponsored programs of artificial birth control, thus ignoring the conscientious convictions of Catholic taxpayers in this important area of public policy.[23]

The joint reply was classified as essentially a "yes" answer to both questions, despite several qualifications.*

* With reference to the word "impose" in line 15 above it should be understood that contraception is self-medication, requiring the consistent cooperation of the patient. At line 16 the signers' declaration with regard to the conscientious convictions of private hospitals recalls the controversy that erupted a decade ago in Poughkeepsie, N. Y. There seven non-Catholic physicians on the staff of St. Francis' Hospital were ordered either to resign from the hospital or sever their connections with the Dutchess County League for Planned Parenthood. Four of the 7 refused to comply, but their staff privileges were restored a year later.

Ten | The World Problem

On July 24, 1959, newspaper headlines read: "Urge U.S. Give Birth Control Data to World." Washington dispatches highlighted an all but buried item in a report of the President's Committee to Study the U.S. Military Assistance Program prepared under the chairmanship of General William H. Draper. The Committee had recommended that the United States: assist the underdeveloped countries, "on request," to formulate plans for dealing "with the problem of rapid population growth"; increase its assistance to local maternal and child welfare programs, and "strongly support studies and appropriate research . . . to meet the serious challenges posed by rapidly expanding populations."[1]

In a sharp comment on the report, the Catholic bishops of the United States declared:

For the past several years a campaign of propaganda has

been gaining momentum to influence international, national, and personal opinion in favor of birth prevention programs. The vehicle for this propaganda is the recently coined terror technic phrase, "population explosion." The phrase, indeed, alerts all to the attention that must be given to population pressures, but it also provides a smoke screen behind which a moral evil may be foisted on the public and for obscuring the many factors that must be considered in this vital question. . . .

The Bishops were confident that "the thus far hidden reservoirs of science and of the earth unquestionably will be uncovered in this era of marvels and offered to humanity." "Catholics" they continued, "are prepared to dedicate themselves to this effort.

They will not, however, support any public assistance, either at home or abroad, to promote artificial birth prevention, abortion or sterilization whether through aid or by means of international organizations.

To give such aid, the Bishops affirmed, would not only promote "a moral evil." It would hinder needed social and economic changes in the underdeveloped countries; would take no account of immigration as a possible solution, and would be bad strategy, both politically and psychologically. What is needed, the Bishops held, is

not to decrease the number of people but to increase the food supply which is almost unlimited in potential.

In conclusion the Bishops said their remarks were "not intended to exhaust this complex subject, nor to discourage demographers, economists, agricultural experts and political scientists in their endeavors to solve the problem." [2]

After the Bishops had spoken, President Eisenhower declared his government would have nothing to do with "this problem of birth control." [3] *

But John F. Kennedy, already a serious contender for the Democratic nomination, said he "would not think it wise for the United States to refuse to grant assistance to a country which is pursuing a policy it feels to be in its own best interest." If Congress were to pass a law making foreign aid contingent on population planning, Mr. Kennedy declared that as president he would base his action on what he "considered to be in the best interest of the United States." [4] When campaigning in 1960, Mr. Kennedy said that while his personal religion was against birth control, "that does not affect my obligation to assume and carry out my oath of office." [5]

Three years later, after he had become President, Mr. Kennedy was asked at his press conference whether he intended to accept the recommendation of the National Academy of Science that this country participate actively in an attack on uncontrolled population growth. The President replied:

> If your question is: Can we do more, should we know more, about the whole reproduction cycle and should this information be made more available to the world so that everyone can make their own judgment, I would think that it would be a matter which we could certainly support.[6]

An amendment to the Foreign Assistance Act of 1963, introduced by Senator J. William Fulbright, provides that

* After he had left office, President Eisenhower reversed his position. In an article entitled "Let's Be Honest with Ourselves," published by *The Saturday Evening Post*, Oct. 26, 1963, he wrote: "The time has come when we must take into account the effect of the population explosion. . . . Population control is a highly sensitive problem, of course. When I was President I opposed the use of Federal funds to provide birth control information to countries we were aiding because I felt this would violate the deepest religious convictions of large groups of tax-payers. As I now look back, it may be that I was carrying that conviction too far. I still believe that as a national policy we should not make birth control programs a condition to our foreign aid, but we should tell receiving nations how population growth threatens them and what can be done about it."

funds be made available for research into the problems of population growth and the inter-relation between economic development and population growth, and that aid and encouragement be given other nations in obtaining needed information on the subject.[7]

Testifying in 1962 on foreign aid before the House Foreign Affairs Committee, the Rev. James L. Vizzard, S.J., Director of the Washington Office of the National Catholic Rural Life Conference, had this to say:

> I don't think . . . we have faced up clearly and courageously to the practical implications for public policy of the deep split between conscientious citizens over what means, if any, may be used in dealing with apparently harmful population growth. . . .
>
> . . . an important public service needs to be performed by bringing together . . . the best minds from all the sciences and . . . efforts would be made to settle on a body of commonly accepted facts. In addition, efforts would be made to enlarge as clearly as possible the area of agreement and to denote as sharply as possible the area of irreconcilable disagreement. . . .
>
> I suggest that if bitter conflict is to be avoided . . . a conflict which can be destructive to our foreign aid program, a proper foundation must soon be laid for the development of public policy on this most delicate and vital issue.[8]

The United States bishops had based their disapproval of governmental aid to other countries wishing to limit population growth on views expressed by Pius XII. On January 20, 1958, in his last address to the Associations of Large Families, Pius XII declared:

> With the progress that has been made in technology, with the ease of transportation, and with the new sources of energy that are just beginning to be tapped, the earth can promise prosperity to all those who will dwell on it for a long time to come. . . .

> So overpopulation is not a valid reason for spreading illicit birth-control practices.[9]

When the World Population Conference met in Rome in September, 1954, Pius XII stressed the need for research. In an address to the Catholic delegates, he said:

> The science of population is young, but it is basic because it is immediately concerned with human life and it can illuminate certain of the gravest individual and social problems. . . . That is why we urge Catholics to take an active part in the research and the efforts which are made in this domain. But we wish that they do this with fidelity to Christian doctrine.[10]

John XXIII, like his predecessor, took an optimistic view.* In his encyclical, *Mater et Magistra,* he said of the population problem:

> . . . the solution is to be found only in socioeconomic progress achieved in a moral atmosphere befitting the dignity of mankind and the immense value of a single human life. Furthermore it must also embrace world-wide cooperation that permits and favors an orderly and fruitful international exchange of useful knowledge, capital and manpower.[11]

Pope John's successor, Paul VI, recognized in his Christmas message of 1963 that the population increase in "starving areas" has not yet been balanced by increase in food production. "Hunger," he noted, "can become a subversive force with incalculable results." But Paul VI warned against remedies that "consist in attacking the very fecundity of life by means that human and Christian ethics must condemn as illicit." Continuing, the Pope declared:

---

* During his brief pontificate John XXIII devoted no encyclical nor allocution to conjugal morality in all its aspects. What he said on the subject, in short addresses and sermons, was in the Church's long tradition.

Instead of increasing the supply of bread on the dining table of the hunger-ridden world, as modern techniques of production can do today, some are thinking in terms of diminishing, by illicit means, the number of those who eat with them. This is unworthy of civilization.[12]

The French sociologist who was an observer for the Holy See at the 1954 World Population Conference, the Rev. Stanislas de Lestapis, S.J., has accused the people of the have-nations of a guilty conscience. In his book, *Family Planning and Modern Problems,* he writes:

. . . our conscience is guilty not only because it dimly realizes that contraception is a form of egoistic calculation, but also because it is not willing to recognize that our national position is one of privilege. Our privileges ought in fact to lead us to sacrifice some of our affluence in the interests of some of the "proletarian" nations. But at this point our unconscious cleverly effects a guilt transference.

We tell ourselves, he continues, that if those irresponsible "prolific" peoples had had the prudence to reduce their fertility, they would be better off.

Thus, by comparing itself with others our guilty conscience becomes clear. Further, by making itself available to teach others . . . it achieves an astounding self-transformation and becomes a conscience free of guilt. Fooled by their own interests, the wealthy nations then consider themselves as models to be imitated. . . . Birth control quite logically partakes of the magic character of the situation and the process of self-deception is complete.

Only when " a universal charity" has aroused and activated men, can proposals for population control be considered "without risk of self-deception," the author concludes:

In other words, when everything has been done to stimulate production, to encourage improved productivity and to promote the best all-round distribution of capital and wealth, then will be time to discuss in an atmosphere of goodwill and charity, the formidable question of eventual limitation of human fertility in any given population group.

In the meantime, Father de Lestapis calls for "a progressive mobilization of the educational forces" of the over-populated nations to develop "the notion of a more premeditated, more human and more altruistic type of procreation." [13]

As to the dimensions of the world population problem, there is substantial disagreement among Catholic scholars both in this country and abroad. The Rev. John J. Lynch, S.J. notes that from the optimistic school "one gets somewhat the impression that the total answer . . . is the relatively facile one of keeping the technological shoulder to the wheel while depending upon biological laws to prevent any intractable population expansion."

Other commentators, Father Lynch continues, "take a more somber view, though one which is far from desperate."

> They concede, first of all, for some areas of the world an already acute problem of inability to provide properly for an ever-increasing population—a situation which will inexorably worsen unless effectual corrective measures are taken.

These writers' proffered solutions call not only for increased productivity and constructive international action. They also, Father Lynch notes, take "into consideration the element of population control"—to be achieved not through illicit forms of birth prevention but through understanding of "responsible parenthood." [14]

Professor George H. L. Zeegers, editor of *Social Kompas,* an international review of Catholic social scientists, writes:

> the world-population problem forms the first world problem in history, as far as phenomena are concerned, the implica-

tions of which are of direct importance to the welfare of universal humanity.[15]

"Every second one more man is born into the world," writes the Rev. Clement J. Mertens, S.J., of the Faculty Saint Albert de Louvain, Belgium. Referring to the 45 million children who are born every year throughout the world, Father Mertens asks in an article in *Cross Currents:*

> How will these children who ceaselessly enter the world be received? . . . How, in countries with heavy population, often already living in destitution, will the necessary resources be found to educate this ever more numerous youth, to guarantee it later employment and a minimum of security in the face of the hazards of existence?

In countries, he continues, where the population is growing rapidly, particularly in those awakening to economic development, we find "what has been very expressively termed 'the revolution of rising expectations.' Once having known the standard of living of more advanced peoples . . . the others wish to join them, and without delay. . . ."

Father Mertens points to deficiencies in the seminary training of priests who will be sent out as missionaries. Instruction concerned with marriage is generally limited, he comments, "to the prevention of sins against conjugal morality. . . .

> The broader view of the social good, of the problems which the rapid growth of certain populations presents, the destruction of the old equilibrium between births and deaths, is practically ignored. . . .

"It is the duty of the ecclesiastical authorities in each country," Father Mertens continues, "to face the problem." Sociologists in the best universities should be encouraged to do research on ways of teaching to communicants "responsible procreation" and of resisting "the propaganda opposing Catholic ethics." [16]

Sent by his superiors to the Gregorian University in Rome from 1951 to 1957, Father Mertens founded there a new social institute to train priests in the social sciences.

In a lecture at St. Louis University in 1961, he spoke of people starving today "because of the imbalance between population and resources." Father Mertens conceded he knew of no way of solving such problems in the near future—"even in the next decades." He declared that widespread promotion of "immoral methods of limiting population will not work— would be too expensive and take too long." "Nobody," he added, "can offer an easy solution." [17]

A demographer on the faculty of the Graduate School at Fordham University, the Rev. William J. Gibbons, S.J. considers it indisputable that "the higher birth rate and declining mortality in less developed areas of the world mean rapid population growth in the years ahead." But in his view

> . . . the over-all situation does not call for panic or scare technics which portray imminent danger of "standing-room only." Before that happens—it would take some hundreds of years at 1960 rates of growth—the trends of today will presumably be modified downward. This would come to pass by lowered birth rates and/or higher death and infant mortality rates.

"It is this decline in mortality," Father Gibbons continues, "which has made modern man take another look at child-bearing and its responsibilities. . . . Reproduction for human beings has to be a truly human process. Man is not a mere biological being who reproduces without any relationship to the world around him, to the society in which he lives and to its resources. . . . The emphasis in any acceptable solution . . . must be on *responsible parenthood* and hence on responsible use of sex."

While Father Gibbons foresees real gains in the economic, agricultural and social areas, he concludes:

> There are limits to the resources of the earth, however great the effort and technical advances of the future . . .[18]

Sharing this view, the Paulist Father, Louis McKernan, Associate Editor of the *Catholic World,* writes:

> . . . it would be unwise for us to base our argument against birth control on the shaky premise that food production will everywhere continue to keep out in front of population growth. We have no guarantee that it necessarily will.[19]

Skepticism from within the Church about proposed solutions came out in a colloquy at a population conference held in 1963 by the American Assembly at Arden House. The Rev. Walter Imbiorski, director of the Cana Conference (for marriage counseling) of the Chicago Archdiocese, asked Father Thomas, as a sociologist:

> Would you agree that some of the escape hatches which certain Catholic authors have taken are not realistic? For instance, the idea of migration, the idea of economic growth, the idea of better movement of food— . . . all of these are going to be helpful . . . but . . . they're going to be too late. . . .

Father Thomas replied:

> Yes, and of course they will also throw in the one of total resources in terms of our scientific ability to produce. . . . In general I think that [they] have really been refusing to face the fact that we have reached a stage where people of all cultures are going to have to regulate family size if they're going to continue their present control of health and their control of death.[20]

That the time may have already come for some countries to consider population control is the view of Msgr. George A. Kelly of the Archdiocese of New York. In his most recent book he states:

> In Latin America and many Asiatic countries . . . the
> overpopulation problem is a very real one. . . . In the view
> of this writer there is little doubt that an individual couple
> might properly limit their family size out of consideration
> for the general well-being of their country and that a par-
> ticular national government might recommend prudence
> in child-bearing to young families. We presume, of course,
> that no pressure is used to limit the family's right to be a
> family, and that no immoral means of family limitation are
> suggested.[21]

The Church in Santiago, Chile, has not opposed the use
of the oral contraceptive. This was reported at the conference
held in September, 1963 at the University of Notre Dame.[22]

A Jesuit magazine published in Santiago, *Mensaje,* is reported in the July 14, 1964 issue of *Look* to have asserted in
an article brought out in the late spring: "Taking off from
the base that parents not only have to procreate but make
possible the normal human development of their children,
the Church accepts the regulation of births. It is this that is
called, and rightly so, responsible procreation. Why then not
accept the use of the progestogenes that do nothing but
supplement and carry forward the natural dynamism of
nature?"

Facts about the operation of six contraceptive clinics in the
Chilean capital are reported in an article by Albert Q. Maisel,
published in the April, 1964 issue of *The Reader's Digest.*
He writes that the clinics were set up to prevent abortion as
well as to aid couples in family planning, that all the scientific
methods of birth control are taught, including the rhythm
method, and that "these clinics have met virtually no opposition from the Roman Catholic Church in Chile."

In Rio de Janeiro, at a conference held July 15, 1963 by the
Christian Movement for the Latin American Family, the
Most Rev. D. Halder Camara, Archbishop Coadjutor of the
diocese, urged those in attendance to petition the Ecumenical

Council to make precise definitions of how Catholic families may be limited. He held that married couples should not be asked to submit blindly to the natural law.[23]

Whether Alliance for Progress funds will be provided for family planning clinics in the Latin American countries has not been made clear. Addressing an International Planned Parenthood Federation meeting in Puerto Rico in April, 1964, William D. Rogers, Deputy U.S. Coordinator for the Alliance, stressed "the importance of population to economic and social development under the Alliance." He said:

> We intend to cooperate closely with national governments, indigenous scientific institutions, and educational institutions while respecting their particular cultures and moral values. . . .
>
> Changes of attitudes concerning population growth problems are occurring rapidly in all nations of the world. Responsible groups among persons of all principal religions and ideologies recognize the problem, although genuine differences exist on the means which are morally permissible.

"In Latin America time is of the essence," the Deputy U.S. Coordinator concluded. "Programs and efforts that in one decade might have enormous consequences for the future prospects of a nation, may be too little and too late a decade hence. . . ."[24]

A comprehensive view of the world population problem was presented in *Commonweal's* special issue of June 5, 1964, by Dr. Thomas K. Burch. This Director of Demographic Studies at Georgetown University's Center for Population Research notes that the demographic facts differ from one country and one time to another. "Even in the underdeveloped nations . . . rates of increase differ greatly. . . . Meaningful definitions of problems and suggestions for their solutions must be tailormade, even if the cost seems high in terms of intellectual effort. . . .

> In any case, there is without question a general human need to regulate fertility and to control population growth below the biological maximum. Catholics, therefore, must harmonize this need with the teachings of the Faith. And recent developments within the Catholic community indicate that such a confrontation is finally taking place.

But as Dr. Burch sees it, "the common sense recognition of the need for fertility regulation and population control stands in danger of degenerating" both among Catholics and non-Catholics "into an irrational, quasi-religious faith in birth control as a panacea of human ills. . . ."

Technologists, Dr. Burch comments, focus their attention on the "breakthrough" in fertility control. But what if "a cheap, simple, effective and aesthetically pleasing form of birth control *were* found?" he asks. We should still face "the gigantic task of promoting orderly worldwide social and economic development to raise standards of living to decent levels." [25]

That Vatican II will find it necessary to weigh the population problem in preparing its treatise on "The Church in the Modern World" has been suggested by the Dean of the Georgetown University School of Foreign Service, William E. Moran, Jr., in an article distributed by the *News Service* of the National Catholic Welfare Conference. Printed December 12, 1963 by the *Catholic Herald* of Sacramento, California, under the caption, "Church Must Clarify Stand," the article reads in part:

> We live in a tight little world which through technological developments has become so small there are no longer any far away places. We'll either make it a decent place in which all can live or we'll suffer the consequences. . . .

Dean Moran, who is President of the Catholic Association for International Peace and a Trustee of the Population Reference Bureau, lists the questions which he hopes the Ecumenical Council will answer as follows:

Does the Church agree that rapid population growth is one of the serious problems facing the world, a real problem meriting study and action?

Do Catholics have the right in a plural society to impose their moral standards on others of differing views? Do they have the right to insist that since they do not approve of the use of contraceptives they should not be made available upon request under government programs, at home or abroad?

What methods now known for regulating or inhibiting reproduction are licit? What guidelines in theology or the natural law would apply to the acceptability of methods which might be developed?

Eleven | The Call for Research

> To put it bluntly, the whole world needs something
> that will ring bells or flash lights on the day before
> ovulation! Or better yet, a substance which will cause
> ovulation on a given day.

The words quoted are those of Dr. Paul F. Muller, a professor
of gynecology and obstetrics who serves as Medical Director
of the Pre-Cana (pre-marital counseling) Conference of the
Archdiocese of Indianapolis.* Dr. Muller's blunt call for
research to perfect the rhythm method concluded his review
of a fellow Catholic physician's book. It is quoted from one
of four feature reviews of Dr. John Rock's *The Time Has
Come* in the June, 1963 issue of the magazine *Marriage*.

---

* Chief of service at St. Vincent's Hospital, Indianapolis, Dr. Muller is
Assistant in Obstetrics and Gynecology at Indiana University School of
Medicine and is an Associate Examiner of the American Board of
Obstetrics and Gynecology.

Other Catholic writers have also stressed the great need for research. Two years ago an editorial in *Commonweal* read:

> The private side of the story is well-known. . . . The Church's stand on artificial birth control is a major source of leakage from the Church. Where it is not a source of leakage it causes, without doubt, innumerable *crises de conscience* even among unwavering Catholics. . . .

The *Commonweal* editors observed that the American Catholic Church "has been especially remiss" in all but ignoring "the repeated calls by the Church for a major research effort into problems of population growth." And added:

> The related calls for greatly increased work on moral means of family planning have met with only sporadic and scattered response. . . .[1]

A similar note has been struck by other Catholic laymen. In the Catholic quarterly *Cross-Currents*, William Birmingham observes that Christian couples who do not accept the moral theologian's argument with regard to the natural law, but who "out of love" for the Church "attempt no interference," "see a need for a method of family limitation that increases Christian joy." He continues:

> Anyone who pays mild attention to the demographers knows that there is a compelling social need. Anyone who talks with troubled Catholic parents knows there is a personal need. The latter need I consider the more important. Consciences are crying out.[2]

That the rhythm method, as practiced today, is a somewhat unreliable means of family limitation, is generally agreed. As long ago as 1951, Pius XII expressed the hope that "science will succeed in providing this licit method with a sufficiently secure basis." *

In the thirteen years which have elapsed since then, no

* See p. 22.

"secure basis" has been found by either Catholic or non-Catholic scientists. But today, at least, more is known than formerly about the ovulatory process. The knowledge has come through the development by Dr. Rock and others of the progestin compound, or pill, which can be used either to promote fertility or inhibit conception.

"There seem to be two ways," Dr. Rock writes, "of perfecting the rhythm method so that it might work in all or almost all cases:

> by developing a cheap, simple and accurate home test that any woman could use to *predict* the day of ovulation each month;
> or by developing an equally simple way to *induce* ovulation so that it could be made to occur on a selected day of each menstrual cycle.[3]

Dr. Rock explains that ovulation is triggered by a hormone called LH (luteinizing hormone), which is discharged by the pituitary gland into the bloodstream in increasing amounts during the 14 days before the ovum is released. At present, the amount of LH in the bloodstream can only be tested by a lengthy and expensive analysis of a 24-hour collection of urine. The research problem is to develop a simple home test such as is used for detection of sugar in cases of diabetes. Dr. Rock writes:

> One might even envisage a reactive tablet or piece of paper which, when dropped into the morning urine, would change color in the presence of by-products specific of critical amounts of LH, perhaps of progesterone.

The other possible technique—*induction* of ovulation on a given day—would call for the administration of pituitary hormones. "Already," Dr. Rock reports, "we have had some published statements of success in inducing ovulation in a few women.

Recently at the Yale University Medical School, Dr. Lee Buxton and his associates obtained results similar to those previously reported by others, when they caused five women to ovulate in response to injected gonadotropic hormones. There appeared to be no harmful side-effects.

Should extended investigations confirm these findings, they would be of no practical use, Dr. Rock points out, until biochemists find an animal or synthetic substitute for the extract from human pituitary glands. In the reported experiments, the extract was removed at autopsies.[4]

The fact that a simple ovulation-inducing procedure would be of value in facilitating pregnancies as well as in postponing them by the rhythm method, should be an added inducement to its development, Dr. Rock notes.

So far funds have been lacking for this necessary extensive research and for further research in all aspects of human reproduction. A report prepared by the National Institutes of Health, at first withheld, and finally released to the public on December 29, 1962, disclosed that of $6.1 million expended by private foundations, industry and government in 1962, only $2.8 million came from the N.I.H.[5] *

After the N.I.H. report had been published, Msgr. John C. Knott, the Director of the Family Life Bureau of the National Catholic Welfare Conference called for a stepped-up program of research. Pointing out that such investigations might be expected in time to benefit presently sterile couples and possibly prevent the birth of malformed and retarded children, he declared:

> Much good could come from such basic research. The fact that such information could be used for what we, as Catholics, would consider immoral purposes should not

---

* In a later press release the N.I.H. revised its figure, reporting that it had expended in 1962 $3.4 million on human reproduction studies. *N.Y. Times,* Sept. 10, 1963.

prevent us from supporting those who are seeking the truth.

Rather we, as Catholics, should positively encourage all efforts which have as their goal the unlocking of nature's secrets. Ignorance is more to be feared than truth or even its misuse.[6]

One feature of the N.I.H. report not released was the recommendation of more than a dozen consultant scientists that an additional $16.6 million be made available annually for research in human reproduction, plus $4 million as a non-recurring sum to help finance the creation of eight research centers. The consultants included Dr. Rock and a second Catholic physician. In his book, Dr. Rock states:

There is no private agency, or combination of agencies, which is able or willing to support a program of this magnitude. If it is to be done, it must be done by the U.S. government.

Dr. Rock points out that our government spends $3 million a year just to control hoof and mouth disease in cattle, and $880 million a year to *reduce the death rate* among humans.[7] Yet the study of nature's process in *inducing life* among humans has been all but neglected.

From Notre Dame University the Rev. John A. O'Brien commented in the Catholic magazine, *Today's Family:*

Can any Catholic hesitate longer in joining with his non-Catholic fellow citizens in backing the appeal to have the federal government through the National Institutes of Health launch a crash program covering every phase of human reproduction to find methods of birth regulation suitable for all? [8]

In an earlier article in *Look,* Father O'Brien had called a proposal made by Protestant Episcopal Bishop James A. Pike, "An admirable gesture of friendship and good will." As

Chairman of the Clergymen's Advisory Committee of the Planned Parenthood Federation, Bishop Pike had urged that the N.I.H. launch a research program specifically designed to perfect a variety of birth control methods, rhythm included.

"If that were accomplished," Father O'Brien wrote in *Look*, "Bishop Pike would probably favor in the interests of national unity, concentrating on the rhythm method in our foreign aid to underdeveloped countries." [9]

In an article published on the same date by *Ave Maria* and *The Christian Century*, Father O'Brien recommends that the President call a White House Conference on measures for solving the world's urgent population problems. "It is time," he concludes, "to close ranks, time to end the cold war and to work together as brothers and good neighbors." [10]

The proposal for a broad-scale federally-financed research program in human reproduction has raised doubts in some Catholic quarters. The Rev. John J. Lynch, S.J., of Weston College, writes:

> One cannot . . . agree that it would be permissible for Catholics to encourage or to cooperate actively in research programs or clinical projects calculated to promote, even among those of other religious persuasions, methods of fertility control which we recognize to be objectively contrary to moral law. Reasonable toleration of moral error is not that elastic.[11]

But the Boston *Pilot,* the archdiocesan organ, declares, April 20, 1963, in an editorial:

> Certainly the question of research can take high priority. We must know vastly more than we do about human reproduction and the problems of sterility. The resources presently available for studies of this kind are pitifully small and there are no religious divisions involved in the matter of basic research. . . .
>
> Moreover, we must emphasize again the concern of Catho-

lics for the demographic problems of these times and those anticipated in the future. While Catholics will not compromise their principles on the matter of artificial contraception, and are not expected to, they can make their contributions to the study of this problem from many directions . . . the good of mankind requires that all men of good will join in common cause for a better world.

Work toward the common cause has recently been initiated by Georgetown University in Washington, D.C. Its new Center for Population Research has launched a three-year, $225,000 program financed by the university and the Ford Foundation. The Center represents a modest, but significant step toward the goal urged upon scientists by Pius XII. One of its first objectives will be the development of a simple ovulation test to perfect the rhythm method.[12] To this end the Center has launched a nationwide study of 5,000 Catholic women. It will have the cooperation of the Christian Family Movement, the Family Life Bureau of the National Catholic Welfare Conference, and a third leading Catholic lay group. The survey asks women from 15 to 45 years of age to record their menstrual cycles, which vary with age. In this connection, the Center's former director, Dr. Benedict J. Duffy, told the press:

> If we can determine the length of a "normal" cycle, we can give the priest a criterion to use in judging whether a woman is irregular enough to countenance the use of a drug to make her cycle regular.[13]

The Center's research activities will not necessarily be confined to the rhythm method. The blue-print for its program states that:

> Although presumably there would be a focus on topics of special interest to Catholics, any exclusive focus on such topics would be detrimental to the status of the Center; there is need to foster research on the whole range of ques-

tions connected with human population, whether or not they have any particular connection with Catholicism.[14]

At St. Francis Hospital in Evanston, Illinois, a gynecologist, a specialist in internal medicine, a pathologist and a bio-chemist are at work as a team on their own research project aimed at pin-pointing ovulation. The four scientists, all members of the faculty of Loyola University's Stritch School of Medicine, have carried on their work with limited funds from the National Institute of Health. In an interview distributed by the *News Service* of the National Catholic Welfare Conference in March, 1964, Dr. Bart Heffernan, the internist of the team, is quoted as saying that he first became aware of the need to find an answer for Catholic couples pressed by economic or health reasons to limit their families, when he testified in 1962 before the Illinois Public Aid Commission.

As spokesman for the Catholic Physicians Guild at the hearing, he had opposed the use of tax moneys for contraceptive services to unmarried mothers. A few days later, over coffee, the four scientists talked of the possibility of dating ovulation accurately, and decided to "try to do something about it." They still see a great many problems ahead, but are hopeful—as Dr. Rock has suggested—that "the answer may lie in finding a substance in the urine that can be tested to detect changes just before ovulation." In the interview, Dr. Heffernan pointed out that some years ago the sugar level of urine had to be determined by a laboratory, but now the test is so simple the diabetic can administer it himself.[15]

At St. Vincent's Hospital in New York City a pragmatic research program was initiated in March, 1962 simply to determine whether the rhythm method would work under proper conditions. The two-year project was financed under grants from New York Catholic Charities and an Illinois industrialist, who became interested in the practicality of the rhythm method since he has numbers of Catholic women employees. Describing the project in its March, 1964 issue,

Jubilee reports that of about 300 women patients who have participated in it, only ten have become pregnant. The physicians who instruct and guide the women volunteers in the practice of rhythm attribute the ten pregnancies not to any deficiency in the system, but to "patient failure." That is, the women did not follow the doctors' instructions exactly, did not observe the specified period of abstinence.

The critical need for research to perfect the rhythm method has been underscored also by Cardinal Suenens. Addressing the first Catholic World Congress of Health in 1958 at the Brussels Exposition, the Cardinal made a dramatic appeal to the Christian conscience of the scientists and physicians attending.

> We all know the sad problems faced by so many families who have to space their children's births for economic or medical reasons and who suffer because of this. They know the law of the Church . . . and they want to obey it. But they suffer because they cannot harmonize, I will not say love, but one of its expressions, with this law of God.
>
> We have no right to demand that men obey this law without, at the same time, doing everything we can to make obedience possible, without straining all our energies to make the way clear.
>
> There are some sins of intellectual inertia and laziness which will appear graver than weakness at the Last Judgment.[16]

Twelve | The Future

At this point in the Twentieth Century the birth control controversy has brought the Church to a cross-roads. In his notable pronouncement of June 23rd, 1964 to the cardinals of the Roman Curia, as already noted, Pope Paul VI declared that "the matter is under study, a study as wide and deep as possible. . . ." The Pope observed that "everyone talks about it,"—"the problem of population increase on the one hand and of family morality on the other." "An extremely grave problem," the Pope termed it, one which "touches the sources of human life . . . the sentiments and the interests which are closest to the experience of man and woman." He voiced the hope that the Church's study of the question will soon be finished "with the help of many and eminent scholars"; and stated that the conclusions of the study will be given "in the form which will be considered most adequate to the subject treated and to the aim to be achieved." *

Is it to be expected that the "many and eminent scholars" who are being consulted will advise Pope Paul to formulate some modification of Pius XI's teaching in *Casti Connubii* that no method of birth regulation is moral other than abstinence during the fertile period?

Already, it would appear, a consensus among theologians and clerical leaders is developing on the morality of a still-to-be-scientifically-confirmed oral compound which would not inhibit ovulation but would so regularize the cycle as to reduce to a few days the period of abstinence necessary to ensure against impregnation.

Should clinical studies show such a pill to be reliable, it could be one answer for all those Catholic couples who wish devoutly to follow the Church's teaching, but who complain of the present uncertainties of the rhythm method and of tensions induced by prolonged abstinence. Whether a regularizing pill could be taken safely over a long period of years; and whether it would be useful for family limitation in impoverished, underdeveloped countries are questions still to be answered.

More satisfactory, but also impractical for underdeveloped countries, would be a simple, empirical test by which a woman could easily determine the onset of ovulation—a test which would, as it were, "ring bells or flash lights," to quote again the words of the Catholic gynecologist in Indiana.

Scientists have talked of the feasibility of such a test, but they have so far lacked the necessary funds for an exhaustive research program in human reproduction. Should the United States government make such funds available, it would seem more than likely that a simple home test would in time be devised. In this nuclear age the scientists have made far more amazing discoveries. While their research in space has pushed

* For text of Pope Paul VI's statement see pp. 5 and 86-87.

back the limits of our universe, research in the marvelous and complicated process by which man reproduces himself has been tragically slighted. Once the scientists find the keys that will unlock the secrets of the reproductive process, the way will be open, among other advances, to the correction of sterility, to the salvaging for a normal life of many children now born defective, and to a pinpointing of the time of ovulation which would afford to humans rational control of the generative process. Such a discovery as this would relegate to the past the dispute over approved methods of birth control, leaving each couple free to make their own decision on family size in the light of their religious or moral convictions. Such a discovery, incidentally, would overturn the economics of birth control. For countless women—non-Catholic as well as Catholic —would find a simple home test preferable to either an oral contraceptive or a mechanical device.

Unhappily, the scientists do not as yet have underway extensive research that might be expected in time to simplify the rhythm method and give it, as Pope Pius XII urged in 1951, "a sufficiently secure basis." The Church is therefore proceeding, as Pope Paul VI has announced, with its doctrinal re-examination of the natural law as it bears on licit methods of family regulation. As to the outcome of the study, so eminent a theologian as Father Häring, of the Theological Commission of the Ecumenical Council, writes in the June 5, 1964 issue of *Commonweal*:

> It would be mistaken to expect the Church some day to revoke the teaching of *Casti Connubii* and to teach precisely the contrary. But neither are the requirements of sound theology and pastoral care satisfied by a one-sided adherence to the formulations of that great document of the Church's teaching authority. . . . The encyclical, published nearly thirty-five years ago, at the time constituted a milestone on the road to a more positive spirituality of marriage; but the formulations concerning abuses in mar-

riage were framed with a backward glance at an era which had not yet come to a close, not in anticipation of what was to become an increasingly general attitude and social structure.

"This should not be construed," Father Häring continues, "as a criticism of a teaching document, but rather as a justification against those who interpret it mechanically and want to apply it mechanically, thus bringing it into disrepute."

It is this theologian's view that married couples "who for a certain time are obliged to prevent a new conception and who, in good conscience or not, fail to find the right means, will not automatically be put on a level with Onan. . . ."

Father Häring is confident that "those Christians who know what they mean by responsible parenthood will certainly not subscribe to any defacing of conjugal love by the deliberate perversion of conjugal union." "Any arbitrary violation of the personal realization of conjugal love or of the natural functions must be rejected as a matter of principle. But any moral judgment concerning a mode of conduct must necessarily have regard to the general orientation of people's lives. . . ." [1]

Should the emerging liberal view prevail and the Church's teaching be so qualified that Catholic couples will not be judged to have sinned—or to have gravely sinned—so long as they have remained faithful to the Christian ideal of responsible parenthood, periodic continence will still be held the ideal to be attained whenever possible. Even Father Janssens, whose views on the licitness of the pill when used for moral reasons have aroused great controversy, believes, as previously quoted, that "one should not have recourse to progesterone when the practice of periodic continence is possible and sufficiently efficacious to assure a voluntary and generous procreation." A similar position, the reader will have noted, is taken by the philosopher, Louis Dupré.

While Dr. Dupré stresses "the very complexity" of many cases, he is at one with Cardinal Suenens, Father de Lestapis and the moral theologians when he declares that "authentic *human* love cannot be attained without self-control." But as a philosopher, he goes further and stresses man's need for a clearer understanding of his own sexuality. The same imperative need has been underlined by Father Thomas in his role as a sociologist. Speaking on a panel with clergymen of other faiths before a conference held by Planned Parenthood-World Population on May 1, 1964, Father Thomas said, "As I see it, modern man's new status relating to reproduction requires a thorough reinterpretation of the personal and social significance of human sexuality. . . ." He called for:

> the careful formulation of an integrated view of human sexuality that would take into account not only the complementary character of its physiological, psychological and spiritual attributes, together with the various stages of its growth in the process of personality development, but also the individual and institutional implications of its function as a unique means of expressing human love and creativity.[3]

It would be appropriate for the Roman Catholic Church, after having had the necessary studies made, to present such an integrated view of human sexuality to contemporary society. For whatever may be said of the negative aspects of the Church's present-day teaching on conjugal morality and procreation—a teaching perhaps not yet entirely free of the Augustinian influence—one truth should be recognized. Through the character of its teaching that marriage is a sacrament symbolizing Christ's union with the Church, it has more successfully than any other faith imbued its communicants with a spiritual ideal of marriage.

The deep study which Catholic scholars are giving to all the moral and even practical aspects of the birth control question and the range of views reported in these pages should disabuse non-Catholics of the image many have held of the Roman Catholic Church as a static, completely authoritarian institution which tolerates neither freedom of speech nor freedom of thought. The Church's history shows that it does reevaluate and develop its teachings at epochal periods. That it is going through such a period today, a period of "opening its windows to the world," in the words of the late Pope John XXIII, is evident.

One significant change has been the admission of laymen to at least the periphery of the sessions of Vatican II. Still more significant has been the assumption, during the 1960's, by a growing number of the unordained, of a right which they consider a duty, to speak out as devout Catholics who wish to see their Church in fact "renew" itself.

Yet another sign of a changing climate within the Church is the public expression of views by priests, who, like Msgr. Casey, write candidly of their "pastoral dilemma" in being obliged to counsel overburdened parents that the only moral method of family limitation is the not easily followed rhythm method.

A concept of conjugal morality that they see as at once consonant with the Christian ideal and with the radically altered living conditions of the latter part of this century, has been urged by a substantial number of Catholic writers, including some distinguished clerical scholars. Yet these writers who recognize the dimensions of the problem as it affects the individual family and countries with rapidly expanding populations, expect no sweeping or hurried changes. For they know that their Church is a great universal institution which must eschew undue haste in any revision of its moral teachings, regarding mankind, as it does, "under the aspect of eternity."

ADDENDUM

At the Ecumenical Council, the long-awaited debate on moral methods of family limitation broke into the open on October 29, 1964. In the course of discussion of the *schema* on "The Church in the Modern World," Paul-Emile Cardinal Léger of Montreal took the floor to point out that confessors the world over are confronted by people who have difficulty with the Church's teaching on marital sex. He held a rethinking of the Church's theology of marriage to be the most urgent requirement and concluded that when this has been accomplished "on the level of principle, moralists, physicians, and psychologists will be in a position to take care of other details."

Cardinal Suenens declared that the Catholic outlook has become too one-sided; that the emphasis on the Biblical command to Adam and Eve to "increase and multiply" must be balanced with the implications of their becoming "two in one flesh", and that the Church's unwillingness to act in this matter could turn out to be "another Galileo case". The Belgian cardinal accordingly called on the Council to set up its own commission to work with the study group already appointed by Pope Paul VI, and urged that the names of commission members be made public.

His Beatitude Maximos IV Saigh, the Melkite Patriarch of Antioch, Syria, asserted that the Church's main problem is to find "the courage" to look at the issue. Its traditional teaching, he declared, may even be the result of "a bachelor psychosis" found among the clergy. At stake, he declared, "is the future of the Church's mission in the world." *

The Syrian cardinal pointed to the "gap" between the Church's official doctrine and the actual practice of many Catholics who "find themselves forced to live in rupture with the law of the Church, far from the sacraments, in constant anguish, because of the inability to find the viable solution between two contradictory imperatives: conscience and normal conjugal life." In this connection, Cardinal Léger called for a new recognition of the importance of conjugal love as an essential element in marriage and "a good in itself". †

During the debate, which was cut off by a standing vote on October 30, Alfredo Cardinal Ottaviani of the Roman Curia, declared that granting couples the right to determine the number of their children, even within current stringent Church rules, was "unheard of in past ages". The Archbishop of Palermo, Sicily, Ernesto Cardinal Ruffini, held that the draft of the *schema,* which had been criticized as too timid in its approach to marriage problems, was dangerous in that it left too much to the discretion of individuals.

"Intrinsically evil means" of limiting offspring were condemned by Bernard Cardinal Alfrink of Utrecht. But the Dutch prelate stressed that "among married people, scientists and some theologians, an honest doubt has arisen regarding the arguments used to prove that in . . . conflicts in the married life of the faithful of good will, complete or periodic continence is the only efficacious, moral and Christian solution possible." ‡

Commenting to the press on October 29, the editor of the Westminster *Clergy Review,* the Rev. Charles Davis, who is dogmatic theologian at St. Edmund's Seminary, Ware, England, declared: "Today represents a turning point whose impact can hardly be overestimated. . . . Now the suggestion has been made in the Council of a re-thinking—not on the [progestin] pill only—but on the whole general doctrine on marriage. The authority of the speakers today shows it can be said those who think a change is needed, have support." *

* *Catholic Star Herald,* Camden, N.J., Nov. 6, 1964
† *Commonweal,* editorial, Nov. 13, 1964
‡ *New York Times,* Oct. 30, 31, 1964

Appendix | Data on Medical Safety of
Oral Contraceptives

An OUTRIGHT challenge to the pill's medical safety was published in 1962 by the National Catholic Welfare Conference, in the form of a leaflet entitled *Oral Contraceptives: A Medical Critique*. Signed by Dr. Herbert A. Ratner, Director of Public Health of Oak Park, Illinois, the leaflet quotes physicians on medical problems which may be associated with the use of the pill and on its as yet unknown long-term effect. The NCWC pamphlet also raises the question whether women who use the oral contraceptive may be more vulnerable than others to thrombophlebitis.

Since there had been reports of deaths due to thromboembolism among users of Enovid, the Food and Drug Administration, in January, 1963, empaneled an *ad hoc* committee of ten medical authorities to evaluate a possible causal relation. With Dr. Irving Wright of New York City serving as chairman, the panel included specialists in gynecology and obstetrics, vascular diseases, thromboembolism, hematology, statistics, and epidemiology. The Committee's final report dated September 12, 1963, stated:

> In summary: on the basis of the available data . . . no significant increase in the risk of thromboembolic death from the use of Enovid in this population group has been demonstrated.
>
> There is a need for comprehensive and critical studies regarding the possible effects of Enovid on the coagulation balance and related production of thromboembolic conditions. Pending the development of such conclusive data and on the basis of present experience this latter relationship should be regarded as neither established nor excluded. Although a detailed study is not within the scope of this report it is recognized that in judging the over-all risk from and the values of the use of Enovid, data concerning the risks of pregnancy and induced abortion in each group would be extremely important.

When the Wright Committee's report was first issued on August 4, 1963, the beginning paragraph of the summary included two additional sentences which read: "The relative risk, from the available data, of death from thromboembolism does appear to be increased for Enovid users at ages 35 or over. The reasons for this are not clear at this time." These were deleted in the final report, since, it was announced, a statistical error had been made in comparing the 35-and-over Enovid users with the general population group. The FDA accordingly, on September, advised the manufacturer, G. D. Searle and Company, that the labelling of the drug, as requested by the agency in August "may be modified to state the higher rate of fatalaties [in the age-group over 35] is not statistically significant." Left unaltered was the FDA's August 4th order to the manufacturer to advise physicians that the "principal contraindications for use of Enovid as a contraceptive" are "certain cancers, pre-existing liver dysfunction or disease, and a history of thrombophlebitis or pulmonary embolism." Left unchanged, also, was the FDA's statement, in its release of August 4, that "Enovid is only recommended for short-term use (2-4 years), primarily where pregnancy is contraindicated."

The Wright Committee had found it impossible to determine whether Enovid-takers run a greater risk of nonfatal thrombophlebitis than do other women of comparable age-groups because of "the large number of unhospitalized and medically untreated cases." The Committee did, however, study the case histories of 5,789 Enovid users, obtaining data from 20 private gynecologists and obstetricians and from six Planned Parenthood Centers. Among these women, 92 percent of whom were under 40 years of age, the incidence of reported phlebitis was 1.55 per thousand, and of pulmonary embolism, .34 per thousand—two cases which did not prove fatal.

Since Enovid produces some uterine conditions similar to those occurring in pregnancy, coagulation changes during this period were reviewed, the Committee noting that thromboembolism occurs "four to six times more frequently" immediately after delivery than at any time before. After making a comparative study of coagulation changes among a limited number of Enovid-users, the Committee stated:

> The available data to date do not establish, or exclude, the possibility that the drug produces hypercoagulability. . . . More complete and extensive studies in this area are clearly needed. Moreover, the question of the relationship of the hypercoagulable state . . . to clinical thromboembolic disease is still undetermined.

The Committee of course studied the 14 thromboembolic deaths reported in 1961 and 1962 among Enovid users, which were "not ascribable to a post-operative state, cancer, pregnancy, extreme obesity, or prolonged dependency edema."

Since ten had occured in 1962, these were compared with thromboembolic deaths not attributable to any of the causes mentioned, which had been reported in like age groups of women. To make a statistical comparison, the Committee assumed that one million women had used Enovid in 1962, having adjusted downward the manufacturer's figure of 1,300,000 prescriptions filled. The adjustment was made to allow for an unknown number of duplicate prescriptions and for an X-ratio, among the Enovid users, of Negro women, who were excluded from the analysis since no Negro user of Envoid was reported to have died of thromboembolism. The Committee's computations showed the rate of incidence of fatal thromboembolism among Enovid users to be 12.1 per million, and the general population rate, adjusted for age distribution, to be 8.4. This difference the Committee found "not statistically significant. . . ."

Since the number that was used of estimated Enovid-users was not an exact one, the Committee made some attempt to estimate the effect of a 50 percent decrease, or alternatively, of a 10 percent decrease in the estimated number. It concluded that a 50 percent decrease in the total number of users was "highly unlikely," but that a 10 percent decrease in the "user population estimate . . . might represent a reasonable error." Such a decrease, its report states, would "*not* yield Enovid-user death rates significantly different from the general population rates. . . . " (Wright committee Report to FDA, Sept. 12, 1963; FDA releases, Aug. 4, Sept. 20, 1963)

Asked in June, 1964 whether the "comprehensive and critical study" recommended by Dr. Wright's Committee had as yet been initiated, the Medical Division of the FDA said the agency is relying on the continuing research program being carried on by the Planned Parenthood-World Population Centers in this country. To date 7,000 Enovid-users have been enrolled in this research program, which calls for a complete medical check every six months.

Studies are in progress at several institutions on laboratory animals to determine whether ingestion of Enovid is related to the incidence or development of cancer or thromboembolism. These studies have so far been negative, with the exception of a University of Oregon Medical School study reported to the American Medical Association's annual convention in late June, 1964, and previously published in abstract in the *AMA Journal* of May 4, 1964. The Oregon study showed that cancer which had been induced in rats was accelerated in growth by the administration of Enovid.

In a comment quoted by the *N.Y. Times* of June 18, 1964, Dr. Charles B. Huggins, Director of the Ben May laboratory for cancer research at the University of Chicago—a pioneer in studies in the relation between hormones and cancer, said the data on women to date indicated definitely that the oral contraceptives were not associated with cancer and that rats are in a different category. At the Worcester Foundation for Experimental Biology in Shrewsbury, Mass. where the oral contraceptive was developed, Dr. Ralph Dorfman said it had been known that hormones under some conditions could affect animal cancers, but that this had not been found to be true in humans. Dr. Dorfman stated there had never been a sign of increased incidence of cancer among the women on whom the pills had been tested, a group of nearly 10,000 over a period of up to eight years. Experience in humans indicates, if anything, Dr. Dorfman added, that the pills protect women against cancer, although this opinion is now receiving further study.

It should be noted that Enovid was chosen for study by the FDA's advisory panel in January, 1963, because it was the first (1960) oral contraceptive to have been approved by the agency, and had been the most widely used. The four other contraceptive pills approved as of Sept., 1964, for prescription by physicians are also progestin compounds. It seems reasonable to suggest that not only Enovid but all the oral contraceptives prescribed with the approval of the FDA should be scrutinized in the course of the "comprehensive and critical" long-term studies which the agency's medical advisory committee recommended.

Bibliography of Principal Sources

America

Bailey, Derrick Sherwin. *Sexual Relation in Christian Thought.*
New York: Harper, 1959

Barrett, Donald N., Ed. *The Problem of Population: Moral and Theological Considerations.* Notre Dame, Ind.: University of Notre Dame Press, 1964

Bekkers, Msgr. W. "Bishop Bekkers on Conjugal Life." Text of TV speech of Mch. 21, 1963; excerpts from *Analecta. Herder Correspondence,* Oct. 1963, pp. 28-30

Catholic press

Catholic Bishops of the United States. Statement, "Explosion or Backfire?" signed in their name by the Administrative Board of the National Catholic Welfare Conference, Nov. 26, 1959, Washington, D.C.

The Commonweal

Cross Currents

de Lestapis, Stanislas, S.J. *Family Planning and Modern Problems.* Tr. Reginald F. Trevett, New York: Herder and Herder, 1961

Duhamel, Joseph S., S.J. *The Catholic Church and Birth Control,* New York: Paulist Press, 1963

Dupré, Louis, *Contraception and Catholics: A New Appraisal*. Baltimore-Dublin: Helicon, 1964

Dutch Bishops. Statement of August 10, 1963 on the oral contraceptive, *America,* April 18, 1964; May 23, 1964

Ford, John C., S.J. and Kelly, Gerald, S.J. *Contemporary Moral Theology*. Vol. II: *Marriage Questions*. Westminster, Md.: The Newman Press, 1963

Farraher, Joseph J., S.J. "Notes on Moral Theology," *Theological Studies,* Vol. 24, No. 1. Mch. 1963, pp. 84-85

Gibbons, William J., S.J., Ed. *Population, Resources and the Future*. "Population and Moral Responsibility." New York: The Paulist Press, 1961

Häring, Bernard, C.Ss.R. Interview with the Rev. John A. O'Brien. "Christian Marriage and Family Planning." *The Problem of Population: Moral and Theological Considerations*. Ed. Donald N. Barrett. Notre Dame, Ind.: University of Notre Dame Press, 1964
———, "Responsible Parenthood," Tr. Mary Ilford, *Commonweal,* June 5, 1964
———, "Theology of Parenthood: Expert Clarifies Views," *Catholic Reporter,* Kansas City, Mo., May 29, 1964

Heenan, Archbishop John C. Statement issued for Bishops of England and Wales. *Catholic Reporter* (London RNS), May 15, 1964

Jubilee

Janssens, L., S.T.D. et Mag. "Morale Conjugale et Progesterones." *Ephemerides Theologicae Lovanienses,* t.39, fasc. 4, 1963

Kelly, Gerald, S.J. "Confusion: Contraception and 'the Pill,'" *Theology Digest,* Vol. 12, No. 2, Summer, 1964, pp. 123-130. *See also* Ford and Kelly

Kelly, Msgr. George A. *The Catholic Marriage Manual*. New York: Random House, 1958
———, *Birth Control and Catholics*, Garden City, N. Y.: Doubleday, 1963
———, "Responsible Parenthood." *America,* May 5, 1962

Kerns, Joseph E., S.J. "Relevant Currents in the History of Sexuality." *The Problem of Population: Moral and Theological Considerations*. Edited by Donald N. Barrett. Notre Dame, Ind.: University of Notre Dame Press, 1964.
———, *The Theology of Marriage: The Historical Development of Christian Attitudes toward Sex and Sanctity in Marriage*. New York: Sheed and Ward, 1964

Lynch, John J., S.J. [on population problem] *Theological Studies.* June, 1960, Vol. 21, No. 2, 227-228
———, Review of Dr. Rock's book. *Marriage,* June, 1963
———, *Catholic Theological Society Proceedings,* 1958, p. 135

McCormick, Richard A., S.J. "Anti-Fertility Pills." *The Homiletic and Pastoral Review,* May, 1963

———, "Conjugal Love and Conjugal Morality." *America,* Jan. 11, 1964

Mertens, Clement J., S.J. "Population and Ethics: Pinpointing the Problem," *Cross Currents,* Summer, 1960

O'Brien, John A. "Let's Take Birth Control Out of Politics," *Look,* Oct. 10, 1961

———, "Dr. Rock's Views on Birth Control." *Today's Family,* Onamia, Minn., Aug. 1963

———, "Let's End the War Over Birth Control," *Ave Maria* and *The Christian Century,* Nov. 2, 1963

Old and New Testament—Douay version

O'Leary, Michael. Letter to *Jubilee,* Mch. 1964

———, "Non-Thought Slams the Door on Truth," *Catholic Star Herald,* April 3, 1964. Reprinted from *The Michigan Catholic,* Mch. 26, 1964

Ottaviani, Cardinal Alfredo, "Vatican Prelate Asks Halt to Statements About Pill Until It Can Be Studied." *Catholic Star Herald* (Vatican City), May 29, 1964

Pope Pius XI. Encyclical Letter, *Casti Connubii—On Christian Marriage.* Dec. 31, 1930. New York: The Paulist Press, 1941

Pope Pius XII. *Marriage and Childbirth.* Address to the Italian Catholic Union of Midwives, Oct. 29, 1951. Tr. by the Very Rev. Canon G. D. Smith. *The Clergy Review,* New Series, Vol. 36, No. 6, and Vol. 37, No. 1. (Dec. 1951-Jan. 1952.)

Pope Pius XII. *Morality in Marriage.* Address to the National Congress of the Family Front and the Directors of Associations of Large Families, Nov. 26, 1951. *The Catholic Mind.* New York: The America Press, 1952

Pope Pius XII. Address to Catholic delegates to Congress on World Population, Sept 9, 1954. *The Catholic Mind.* New York: The America Press, 1955

Pope Pius XII. "The Large Family." Address to the Directors of Associations of Large Families of Rome and Italy, Jan. 20, 1958. *The Pope Speaks,* Vol. IV, No. 4, Spring, 1958, p. 367

———. "Morality and Eugenics." Address to the 7th International Hematological Congress, Rome, Sept. 12, 1958. *The Pope Speaks.* Vol. VI, No. 4, p. 395.

Pope John XXIII. Encyclical Letter. *Mater et Magistra—Christianity and Social Progress,* May 15, 1961. New York: The America Press, 1961

Pope Paul VI. Address to the cardinals of the Roman Curia, June 23, 1964. June 23, 1964 *News Service of the National Catholic Welfare Conference,* June 26, 1964

———. "Christmas Message to the World," *N.Y. Times,* Dec. 24, 1963

Ruether, Rosemary, "A Catholic Mother Tells 'Why I Believe in Birth Control,'" *The Saturday Evening Post,* April 4, 1964

Rock, John, M.D. *The Time Has Come.* New York: Alfred A. Knopf, 1963

Schillebeeckx, E., O.P., quoted in Amsterdam dispatch of N.C.W.C. *News Service,* Mch. 13, 1964

———, Interview with R. Wessling, C.Ss.R. and Carol Enkelarr, Rome, Dec. 2, 1963. *De Linie,* Brussels, Dec. 20, 1963. Excerpts, "Procreation and Human Dignity," *Commonweal,* June 5, 1964

Suenens, Leon Joseph Cardinal. *Love and Control: The Contemporary Problem.* Tr. George J. Robinson. Westminster, Md.: The Newman Press, 1961

Thomas, John L., S.J. *Marriage and Rhythm.* Westminster, Md.: The Newman Press, 1957

van der Marck, W., O.P. "Fertility Control: An Attempt to Answer an Open Question." *Tijdschrift voor Theologie,* 3rd quarter, 1963, no. 4, pp. 378-414

Wright, Irving, M.D. Chairman. *Report on Enovid* by the *Ad Hoc* Committee for the Evaluation of Possible Etiologic Relation with Thromboembolic Conditions. Submitted to the Food and Drug Administration of the Dept. of Health, Education and Welfare, Washington, D.C. Sept. 12, 1963, offset, 15 pp. with appendix

For quotations from Augustine, Aquinas and Church authorities of previous centuries, the author is indebted to Bailey, Kerns and Janssens.

References

CHAPTER I *The Church's Historic Views . . .*

1. Pope Pius XI, *Casti Connubii*, pp. 2, 17, 18
2. Arthur Vermeersch, S.J. *De Castitate,* Rome: P.U.G. 1921, ed. 2a, p. 224
3. Pope Paul VI, address to cardinals of Roman Curia, June 23, 1964
4. Janssens, pp. 793-808
5. Kerns, "Relevant Currents . . ." pp. 26-27
6. ———, *Theology of Marriage,* p. 9
7. Cf. Mircea Eliade, "Chasteté, Sexualité et Vie Mystique chez les Primitifs," *Mystique et Continence.* Travaux *Scientifiques* du VIIe Congrès International d'Avon. Etudes Carmelitaines. Paris: Desclée De Brouwer et Cie, 1952
8. Kerns, *Theology of Marriage,* pp. 9-12
9. Bailey, pp. 1-2
10. ———, p. 59. For the thought of Augustine, see pp. 19-102 *passim*
11. *De bono conjugali,* c. 10, n. 11
12. *Contra Faustum,* XXII, c. 61
13. *De peccatorum meritis et remissione,* I, c. 29, n. 57
14. *De bono conjugali,* c. 7, n. 6

15. *De nuptiis et concupiscentia,* i, 17
16. i. 8, 9
17. Cf. *De bono conjugali,* X; *Sermones.* cccli. 5
18. *De bono conjugali,* c. 11, no. 12
19. c. 10, p. 11
20. *Sermo,* 292, n. 7; *Contra Julianum.* III c. 21, no. 43
21. *De moribus ecclesiae et manischaeorum,* c. 18, no. 65; *Contra Faustum,* XV, c. 7
22. Janssens, p. 795
23. *De bono conjugali,* iii; *De Sermone Domini in monte,* I, c. 14. n 39
24. *Sermo* li, 13
25. *Epistles* cllii
26. *Contra Faustum,* XV, c. 7
27. XIX, c. 26
28. *De genesi ad litteram,* IX, c. 5, n. 9, c. 7, n. 12; c. 11, n. 19
29. *De nuptiis et concupiscentia* I, 3, n. 19; c. 21, n. 23; *Contra Julianum* III, c. 16, n. 30
30. *De nuptiis et concupiscentia,* I, c. 17, n. 19
31. I, c. 10, n. 11
32. *Sermo* 51, c. 21; *Contra Julianum,* V, c. 46
33. Janssens, p. 802
34. Kerns, "Relevant Currents," p. 32
35. Bailey, p. 42
36. *De bono conjugali* X
37. Bailey, pp. 42-43
38. *Confessions,* VIII, vii, 17
39. For a discussion of the sexual aspects of the *Confessions,* see Bailey, pp. 50 ff.
40. Bailey, p. 53
41. *De grat. Chr. et de pecc. orig.* ii, 38, 43
42. ii, 40, 35; *De civitas Dei,* xiv, 17
43. *De civitas Dei,* xiv, 26, also 23, 24; *De nuptiis et concupiscentia,* ii, 14
44. Bailey, p. 53
45. p. 244
46. *Epist.* xi, 64
47. For a survey of mediaeval sexual thought, see Bailey, pp. 107-166; and Kerns' *Theology of Marriage,* pp. 47-83
48. *De beata Marìa Virginie,* c. 1; c. 4; c. 8 *De sacramentis christianae* fidei, I, 8, 13
49. *Compil.* I, IV, iv 6, 8
50. Kerns, *Theology of Marriage,* p. 65
51. *In Sentences,* IV, xxvi, q, 1, a, 3; *Summa Theologiae,* III Suppl. xlix, 4
52. *Summa Theologiae* III. Suppl. xlix, 1

53. Bailey, p. 136
54. *Summa Theologiae,* I, xcii, 1
55. *De ordine,* ii, 4, 12
56. *Opuscula,* xvi, 14
57. *Summa Theologiae,* II-II, x, 11
58. J. Colet. (tr. and ed. J. H. Lupton) *Exposition of St. Paul's First Epistle to the Corinthians.* London, 1874, pp. 90-91
59. *Concilium Trid.,* sess. 24, c. 1. "De reform. matr." Denzinger-Rahner, pp. 960 f
60. Janssens, p. 805
61. *In 4 Sent.,* d. 31, q. 1, n. 3
62. Janssens, p. 797
63. Dominic Palmiere, S.J., *Tractatus de matriomonio Christiano* Rome: Society for the Propagation of the Faith, 1880. tr. 10, c. 2, p. 289
64. Janssens, p. 800
65. ——, pp. 807-808
66. Pius XII. Address to Midwives, Vol. 37, No. 1, p. 48
67. Janssens, pp. 810-811, 813
68. Kerns, "Relevant Currents . . .", pp. 40-41

CHAPTER II *Responsible Parenthood*

1. Pope Pius XII, Address to Midwives, *Clergy Review,* Vol. 36, No. 6, p. 382
2. ——, p. 382
3. ——, p. 388
4. ——, Address to Congress of Family Front, p. 308
5. ——, p. 311
6. Suenens, pp. 88, 101
7. Bekkers, *Herder Correspondence,* Oct. 1963, p. 28
8. Häring, Notre Dame colloquy, pp. 2-3
9. ——, "Responsible Parenthood," *Commonweal,* June 5, 1964
10. ——, Notre Dame colloquy, p. 6
11. Ford and Kelly, pp. 454-456
12. Thomas, p. 11; 128-129
13. ——, pp. 141-144
14. *Catholic Family Leader,* June, 1961
15. Gibbons, p. 14
16. Kelly, Msgr. George A. *Marriage Manual,* p. 178
17. ——, p. 56, ff.
18. ——, *America,* May 5, 1962
19. *The Pilot,* April 20, 1963
20. O'Brien, *Look,* Oct. 10, 1961
21. de Lestapis, p. 161
22. ——, pp. 212-213

CHAPTER III *The Natural Law . . .*

1. Pope Pius XI, *Casti Connubii,* p. 8
2. "Responsible Parenthood." Statement adopted Feb. 23, 1961 by the National Council of Churches of Christ in the U.S.A., New York, Feb. 23, 1961
3. Statement by Rabbinical Alliance of America, 1958
4. Pope Pius XI, *Casti Connubii,* p. 17
5. Suenens, p. 103
6. Ford and Kelly, pp. 271-272
7. Häring, Notre Dame colloquy, pp. 11-12
8. Paul Anciaux. *Le Sacrement du Marriage.* Louvain: Editions Nauwelaerts. Paris: Beatrice-Nauwelaerts, pp. 230-231
9. Ford and Kelly, pp. 272-273
10. Duhamel, pp. 4-7
11. ———, pp. 16, 12
12. Suenens, pp. 94-95
13. Ford and Kelly, pp. 128-129
14. Häring, Notre Dame colloquy, pp. 8-9; 7
15. ———, pp. 9-10
16. Duhamel, pp. 13-14
17. ———, pp. 22-23
18. de Lestapis, pp. 181-183
19. Duhamel, p. 23
20. de Lestapis, p. 191
21. Häring, Notre Dame colloquy, pp. 16-17

CHAPTER IV *Practice of the Rhythm Method*

1. de Lestapis, p. 181
2. Thomas, p. 160
3. George Barrett, "Catholics and Birth Control: Role of Research," 2nd of 4 articles, *N.Y. Times,* Aug. 6, 1963
4. Thomas, pp. 92-99
5. Suenens, pp. 153-154
6. de Lestapis, p. 102
7. Arthur W. Kane, S.J. "The Temperature Method: A Positive Approach to the Physical and Spiritual Problems of Birth Regulation," *America,* May 2, 1964
8. Thomas, pp. 102-105; 156-163
9. Häring, *The Catholic Reporter,* May 29, 1964
10. Dupré, pp. 77-78
11. William V. D'Antonio, "Conjugal Love, Responsible Parenthood, Population: An Inquiry into the Present State of the Question." *The Catholic Reporter,* April 3, 1964
12. Suenens, pp. 60-63; 82
13. de Lestapis, pp. 169-170

14. Msgr. George A. Kelly, *Birth Control and Catholics*, p. 116
15. Bekkers, *Herder Correspondence*, Oct. 1963, pp. 28-29

CHAPTER V *The Married Speak*
1. Frank M. Wessling, "Is It Immature Loving?" *America*, May 2, 1964
2. John Dietzen, letter to *America*, Nov. 23, 1963
3. Letter, *America*, Nov. 23, 1963
4. St. Gerard's Bulletin, Ligouris, Mo. Jan. 1964
5. "Husband and Wife Report," *America*, Nov. 23, 1963
6. Letter from a psychiatrist, *Jubilee*, June, 1964

CHAPTER VI *Illicit—and Licit—Uses . . .*
1. Pope Pius XII, Address to hematologists, p. 395
2. Pope Pius XI, *Casti Connubii*, p. 21
3. Pope Paul VI. Address to the cardinals of the Roman curia, June 23, 1964
4. *America*, "The Pope's Words," editorial, July 11, 1964
5. Rock, pp. 168-169
6. Pope Pius XII, Address to hematologists, pp. 394-395
7. ———, p. 397
8. ———, Address to midwives, *Clergy Review*, Vol. 36, No. 6, p. 390
9. ———, Address to hematologists, p. 395
10. Ford and Kelly, pp. 358-359
11. John J. Lynch, S.J., *Catholic Theological Society Proceedings*, 1958, p. 135
12. Francis J. Connell, C.Ss.R., *American Ecclesiastical Review*, 143, Sept. 1960, pp. 203-205
13. Denis O'Callaghan, *Irish Theological Quarterly*, 27, 1960, p. 13
14. Ford and Kelly, pp. 351-352
15. Janssens, p. 790
16. Ford, "Priest Says Birth Control Pill Immoral," *N.C.W.C. News Service*, Feb. 21, 1964
17. Häring, Notre Dame colloquy, p. 20
18. Suenens, press interview *Pilot*, May 9, 1964
19. "Drug [Duphaston] May Create Scientific Basis for Rhythm System," *Catholic Reporter*, May 3, 1963
20. Ford and Kelly, p. 360
21. Richard A. McCormick, S.J. "Anti-Fertility Pills." *The Homiletic and Pastoral Review*, May, 1963, pp. 698-699
22. Ford and Kelly, pp. 361-362
23. Häring, *Catholic Reporter*, Apr. 3, 1964
24. Janssens, p. 792
25. Ford and Kelly, pp. 362-363; p. 137

27. Janssens, pp. 791-792

28. Paul Anciaux, "Geboortenregeling en hormonpreparten," *Collectnea Mechliniensia* 30, 1960, p. 17. Quoted in *Collationes Burgenses et Gandavenses,* 1960, p. 134

29. *Studi Cattolici,* Nov.-Dec., 1961. 27. Rome, pp. 62-67

30. Joseph J. Farraher, S.J. "Notes on Moral Theology." *Theological Studies.* Vol. 24, No. 1, Mch. 1963, pp. 84-85

31. Francis J. Connell, C.Ss.R. *N.C.W.C News Service,* Dec. 18, 1961

32. Ford and Kelly, pp. 371-372; 374-375

33. Häring, colloquy at Notre Dame, p. 19

34. Ford and Kelly, p. 345

CHAPTER VII *Controversy Over . . . Pill*

1. *Catholic Star Herald* of Camden. Dispatch from Louvain. "Theologian Contends Birth Control Pill Akin to Rhythm—Belgian's Position Challenged in U.S.," Feb. 28, 1964

2. Janssens, pp. 824, 788

3. Ford, "Priest Says Birth Curb Immoral," *Catholic Star Herald* (NC), Feb. 21, 1964

4. *Catholic Star Herald,* "Some Moral Theologians Rap Theory," Feb. 28, 1964

5. Michael O'Leary, "Non-Thought Slams the Door on Truth," *Catholic Star Herald,* April 3, 1964

6. ———, Letter to *Jubilee,* Mch. 1964

7. Bekkers, *Herder Correspondence,* Oct. 1963, p. 30

8. "The Dutch Bishops on the Pill," *America,* April 18, 1964, p. 531; May 23, 1964, p. 696

9. "Holland Makes Crack in Dike on 'Pills.' " *The Catholic Reporter* (NC), Mch. 13, 1964

10. Schillebeeckx, *Commonweal,* June 5, 1964

11. van der Marck, *Tijdschrift voor Theologie,* 3rd. quarter, 1963, no. 4, pp. 378-414

12. Dupré, p. 69

13. "A Stir in England: Prelate Questions Church's Teaching on Birth Control; Theologians Quickly Rebut," *Catholic Star Herald* (London NC), May 1, 1964

14. "Bishops of England, Wales Renew Condemnation of Pill," *The Catholic Reporter* (London RNS), May 15, 1964

15. "Dutch Bishops . . . and British," *America,* May 23, 1964, p. 696

16. *Pittsburgh Catholic,* editor's reply to letter-writer, Mch. 19, 1964

17. *Catholic Weekly,* Saginaw, Mich. "Debate on the 'Pill' ", editorial by the Rev. Neil O'Connor, editor of the Catholic Weekly editions for Dioceses of Saginaw and Lansing, Mch. 20, 1964

18. *Providence Visitor,* "Birth Control Controversy," editorial, Mch. 13, 1964

19. *Ave Maria,* "Caution Required in Theology Debate," editorial, Mch. 14, 1964

20. *America,* "Time's Bomb," editorial, April 25, 1964

21. *Commonweal,* "What Is the Consensus?" editorial, Mch. 20, 1964

22. *Catholic Star Herald,* "The Pill and the Press," column by Msgr. S. J. Adamo, April 3, 1964

23. *The Catholic Reporter,* "British Bishops on Use of 'Pill,'" editorial, May 15, 1964

24. "Vatican Prelate Asks Halt to Statements About Pill Until It Can Be Studied," *Catholic Star Herald* (Vatican City), May 29, 1964

CHAPTER VIII *Priest, Theologian and Layman*

1. Msgr. George W. Casey, "The Pastoral Crisis," *Commonweal,* June 1964, pp. 317-319

2. "Marriage, Love, Children, Readers' Comments on Aspects of Sex and Marriage," *Jubilee,* June 1964, pp. 27, 28, 31, 20, 17

3. Eldon M. Talley, letter to *Jubilee,* Mch. 1964, p. 42

4. Daniel Callahan, "Authority and the Church," *Commonweal,* June 5, 1964, pp. 319, 323

5. *Commonweal,* editorial, May 17, 1963

6. Häring, Notre Dame colloquy, pp. 19-20

7. Dupré, footnote, p. 86

8. Ford and Kelly, pp. 268-270

9. Dupré, p. 55

10. ———, p. 46

11. Häring, Notre Dame colloquy, pp. 4-5

12. Dupré, p. 46

13. ———, pp. 83-87

CHAPTER IX *Public Policy . . .*

1. Gustav Weigel, S.J., *Catholic Theology in Dialogue,* New York. Harper, 1960, pp. 106, 117

2. O'Brien, "Let's Take Birth Control Out of Politics," *Look,* Oct. 10, 1961

3. John Courtney Murray, S.J., "America's Four Conspiracies." *Religion in America.* Ed. by John Cogley. New York: Meridian Books, 1958, p. 33

4. The Rev. John J. Lynch, S.J., *Theological Studies,* Vol. 21, No. 2, June, 1960, p. 234

5. James O'Gara, "All Things Considered: Birth Control Laws," *Commonweal,* Jan. 26, 1962

6. "Birth Control and Planned Parenthood," *Commonweal,* Aug. 23, 1963

7. The Rev. John Maguire, C.S.C. "Those Anti-contraceptive Laws," *Ave Maria,* June 11, 1960

8. Richard Cardinal Cushing, TV speech as quoted by *Christian Science Monitor,* Feb. 16, 1963, and by George Barrett, *N.Y. Times,* Aug. 7, 1963

9. The Rev. Henry V. Sattler, as quoted by Barrett, *N.Y. Times,* Aug. 7, 1964

10. James Finn, "The Controversy in New York: Morality and Pluralism," *Commonweal,* Sept. 12, 1958

11. O'Brien, *Look*

12. Release from Dr. Ray E. Trussell, Commissioner, N.Y. City Department of Hospitals, July 13, 1964

13. *N.Y. Times,* Jan. 13, 1964

14. *N.Y. Times,* July 13, 1964

15. Personal communication

16. *N.Y. Times,* Jan. 21, 1964

17. *Post-Times-Herald,* Washington, D.C., Mch. 18, 1964

18. Bishop Philip M. Hannan, as quoted in an editorial, *Washington Star,* Mch. 31, 1964

19. *San Francisco Chronicle,* May 19, 1964

20. *N.Y. Times,* Mch. 25, 1964

21. O'Gara, *Commonweal,* Aug. 23, 1963

22. John F. Kennedy, as quoted by *Milwaukee Journal,* Apr. 2, 1960

23. *Planned Parenthood Federation* release on poll of Catholic laymen, Oct. 31, 1962

CHAPTER X *The World Problem*

1. *Economic Assistance Programs and Administration,* Report to President Eisenhower of Committee to Study the U.S. Military Assistance Program, Chairman, General William H. Draper, July 23, 1959, pp. 96-97

2. Catholic Bishops of the U.S. Statement. *N.C.W.C. News Service,* Nov. 26, 1959

3. *N.Y. Herald Tribune* (UPI) Dec. 3, 1959

4. *N.Y. Times,* Nov. 26, 1959

5. John F. Kennedy, address at Bethany College, W.Va. Apr. 18, 1960

6. ———, press conference, Apr. 25, 1963

7. *Foreign Assistance Act of 1963.* 88th Congress, H.R. 7885. Public Law 88-205. Enacted Dec. 16, 1963

8. James L. Vizzard, S.J. Statement on the Foreign Assistance Act of 1962. Before the House Foreign Affairs Committee. Released by the *National Catholic Rural Life Conference,* Apr. 18, 1962

9. Pope Pius XII. Address to the Associations of Large Families, Jan. 20, 1958, p. 367

10. ———, Address to World Population Congress, Sept. 9, 1954, p. 256

11. Pope John XXIII. *Mater et Magistra*, p. 53

12. Paul VI, "Christmas Message to the World," *N.Y. Times*, Dec. 24, 1963

13. de Lestapis, pp. 279-280; 282, 268

14. Lynch, *Theological Studies*, June, 1960 Vol. 21, No. 2, 227-228

15. George H. L. Zeegers. "The Meaning of the Population Problem." *Cross Currents*, Winter, 1958, p. 19

16. Mertens, *Cross Currents*, Summer, 1960, pp. 267-268; 278-279

17. "Birth Rate Specialist Predicts 'Rethinking,' " *The Pilot* (NC), Oct. 7, 1961

18. Gibbons, "Population and Moral Responsibility." *Population, Resources and the Future*, pp. 9-10; 15; 18-20

19. Louis McKernan, C.S.P. "Population in a Changing World." *Population, Resources, and the Future*, p. 26

20. *N.Y. Times*, Aug. 6, 1963

21. Msgr. George A. Kelly, *Birth Control and Catholics*, pp. 195-196

22. Donald N. Barrett, Ed. *The Problem of Population . . .* , p. 137

23. *Ode Sao Paulo*, July 15, 1963

24. William D. Rogers, Deputy U.S. Coordinator, Alliance for Progress Agency for International Development. Address before the Western Hemisphere Conference, International Planned Parenthood Federation, San Juan, Puerto Rico, April 19, 1964

25. Thomas K. Burch, "Population and Parenthood." *Commonweal*, June 5, 1964, pp. 328-331

CHAPTER XI *The Call for Research*

1. *Commonweal*, "Family Planning," editorial, Oct. 20, 1961

2. William Birmingham, "The Testimony of Dr. Rock," *Cross Currents*, Spring, 1963

3. Rock, p. 188

4. ———, p. 190-191

5. *A Survey of Research in Reproduction related to Birth and Population Control (as of December, 1962)*, U.S. Department of Health, Education and Welfare, Dec. 29, 1962

6. The Rev. John C. Knott. Statement released by the *National Catholic Welfare Conference News Service*, Dec. 31, 1962

7. Rock, pp. 196-199

8. O'Brien, *Today's Family*, Onamia, Minn. Aug. 1963

9. ———, "Let's Take Birth Control Out of Politics," *Look*, Oct. 10, 1961

10. O'Brien, "Let's End the War Over Birth Control," *Ave Maria* and *The Christian Century*, Nov. 2, 1963

11. The Rev. John J. Lynch, S.J., review of Dr. Rock's book, *Marriage*, June, 1963

12. *N.Y. Times*, Aug. 6, 1963

13. ———, Sept. 27, 1963

14. ———, Aug. 6, 1963

15. Arthur Southwood. "Four Doctors Conduct Studies on Ovulation." *New World* (NC), Chicago, Ill., Mch. 6, 1964

16. Suenens, pp. 149-150

CHAPTER XII *The Future*

1. Bernard Häring, C.Ss.R. "Responsible Parenthood," *Commonweal*, June 5, 1964, pp. 327-328

2. John L. Thomas, S.J., Address delivered at a symposium, "How Can All Churches Work Together for Family Planning?" during a Planned Parenthood-World Population Conference in Dallas, Texas, May 1, 1964. Press release.

Index